Kathy Watson

KEITH DOUGLAS

COLLECTED POEMS

by the same author

*

SELECTED POEMS
ALAMEIN TO ZEM ZEM

Keith Douglas, Western Desert

Keith Douglas

COLLECTED POEMS

EDITED BY
JOHN WALLER, G. S. FRASER AND J. C. HALL

WITH AN INTRODUCTION BY
EDMUND BLUNDEN

CHILMARK PRESS
New York

Published in New York by Chilmark Press, Inc. and
distributed by Random House, Inc.

Library of Congress Catalog Card Number: 66-24374

Second Printing

Printed in The United States Of America

CONTENTS

Army: England

The Middle East

ILLUSTRATIONS

EDITORS' PREFACE

Keith Castellain Douglas was born at Tunbridge Wells, Kent, on 24th January, 1920. His ancestry was Scots-Irish on his father's side and mixed-European (mainly French) on his mother's. In a letter written to Mr. Maurice Wollman, his mother, Mrs. Marie J. Douglas, has told how 'from an early date Keith shewed interest in art. First, shapes intrigued him. Then words. (He started to draw things at two years old.) Always very independent, he usually spurned advice till his own mistakes had proved him wrong. He had few "advantages" in the generally accepted sense of the word and as a baby had to spend long spells on his own. But he was never at a loss for amusement. He "talked" stories to his various toys till he learned to write and then he attempted to write them. He drew on every available scrap of paper; on doors and walls and any soft flat surface he could find in the garden which he could scrape with a stick. He pored over books he couldn't possibly read, comparing shapes of words he knew with shapes he didn't know and trying to guess their meanings.'

His first boarding school was Edgeborough at Guildford, to which he went at the age of six. He could then read and write fluently. His favourite books were an old *History of the Boer War* and the *Children's Encyclopedia*, from which he chose myths, fairy tales and historical anecdotes. A little later he became particularly interested in James Stephens's *The Demi-Gods* and made several attempts to illustrate it.

When Douglas was eight his father left the family, and father and son never saw each other again. From then on Mrs. Douglas brought up Keith single-handed, often in very difficult circumstances.

At eleven Douglas proceeded to Christ's Hospital on the Nomination Exam. While there he published his first poems in the school magazine and at the age of sixteen had the distinction of having one ('Dejection') accepted by Geoffrey Grigson for *New Verse*. His mother has written of him at this period: 'He had too much individuality to be popular with many of the Powers—but there were those

13

who appreciated him despite the headaches he sometimes caused. He was impatient of most people's opinions till he had tested them personally. He loved an argument and would cheerfully argue against his own opinions and (theoretically) prove them wrong, rather than have no basis of argument. He did this so convincingly that people who did not know him well sometimes believed his views to be the exact opposite of what they were.

'He was accused by the Headmaster of being constitutionally lazy. The truth was he had unbounded energy and perseverance in anything he considered really worth-while. He was keen on rugger and swimming, on riding, on dancing and acting. He was interested in people and the reasons for their behaviour; in past ages—and the future.'

In October 1938 Douglas went up to Merton College, Oxford, on a scholarship, to study English Literature. His tutor was Edmund Blunden, who in his Introduction to this volume gives us an affectionate impression of his pupil. Douglas took an active part in the literary life of the university, editing *Cherwell* and publishing his work in that and other magazines. Among his contemporaries were Sidney Keyes, John Heath-Stubbs, Herbert Howarth, Margaret Stanley-Wrench, and two of the editors of the present volume, John Waller and J. C. Hall. The Slade School of Art had been evacuated to Oxford on the outbreak of war, and Douglas was able to join its classes and so get his first training as an artist.

Having joined the Oxford O.T.C., largely for the free riding it offered, Douglas was liable for active service as soon as war was declared. His calling-up was delayed, however, and so he enjoyed the year 1939–40 at Oxford. Once in the army he was posted in turn to Edinburgh, Weedon, Sandhurst and Lulworth Cove. After receiving his commission he was eventually selected for special duties with the Indian Army; but the Indian plan was cancelled and Douglas—in default of any particular instructions—went out to the Middle East. He sailed in June 1941 and on arrival was transferred to the Notts Sherwood Rangers Yeomanry.

Douglas's experiences in the Middle East are vividly described in his war journal, *Alamein to Zem Zem*.[1] All that need be mentioned here is that he ran away from a staff job at the base to rejoin his regiment in the desert, and fought in a Crusader tank from Alamein to Wadi Zem

[1] Editions Poetry London (1946). Reissued by Faber and Faber (1966), as a companion to the present volume.

Zem in Tunisia—with the exception of a short period in hospital in Palestine after being blown up by a mine. While in Cairo Douglas met for the first time a number of poets—Bernard Spencer, Lawrence Durrell, Terence Tiller, and one of the editors of this volume, G. S. Fraser—who, like him, were contributing to *Personal Landscape*, a magazine being published in Cairo at that time.

Douglas was now beginning to make his mark as a poet. In 1941 a small selection of his poems had appeared in *Eight Oxford Poets* (Routledge). This was followed in 1943 by a larger selection in a book he shared with John Hall and Norman Nicholson (John Bale & Staples). From the Middle East he sent back many of his poems to friends in England, and these were mostly published by Tambimuttu in *Poetry London*.

Douglas returned from the Middle East just before Christmas 1943 to train for the Second Front. In the following months he spent what time he could collecting together his poems for a volume which he planned to call *Bête Noire*. 'I can't afford to wait', he wrote to Tambimuttu, 'because of military engagements which may be the end of me.' This premonition was realized only too soon. On his third day in Normandy, on 9th June, 1944, Douglas was killed at the age of twenty-four, after getting information from behind the enemy lines for which he was mentioned in despatches.

In a letter to Mr. Maurice Wollman, Douglas's mother has written: 'His last completed poem ["On a Return from Egypt"] reflects, I think, his doubts and urges—his longing to carry out the things he once planned and looked forward to—all the writings, illustrations, back-cloths . . . all the travel. And through all, the sense that if he did not face and share in every experience that came his way neither could he write any more. So for him there was no other choice despite his fear. So he went. He might have stayed in a safer spot. But I understood he couldn't. He always loathed the "safety first" idea, holding that one might as well be dead as afraid to move. He believed in venturing and having—or losing if need be. If he had lived to be a thousand I think he would still have gone on trying to weave his gathered experiences and knowledge into some comprehensible pattern of words and shapes —or sounds.'

The collection Douglas was planning just before his death was never published as such. It was not until 1951 that Editions Poetry London brought out his *Collected Poems*, edited by John Waller and G. S.

Fraser. That edition forms the basis of the present one, with some important differences.

Whereas the poems in the 1951 edition were arranged roughly in reverse chronological order (the idea being to put the emphasis on Douglas's most mature work), they are now arranged in normal chronological order. It must be emphasized, however, that there is still an element of guesswork about this, particularly in regard to the early poems. We have found it convenient to present under the single heading of SCHOOLDAYS all the poems Douglas probably conceived before going up to Oxford. Although he revised and first published some of them only after arriving at Oxford, their essential inspiration and technical skill certainly belong to his schooldays.

A few poems have been transferred to other sections where they seem more appropriately to belong. As indicated in the NOTES, some textual revisions have been made. In the MIDDLE EAST section, a hitherto uncollected poem, 'The Trumpet', is now included; also a new version of 'Landscape with Figures', with the addition of a third section. The NOTES to the 1951 edition have been revised where necessary.

The present edition also differs from its predecessor in containing a selection from Keith Douglas's own illustrations for his poems. The illustration for 'Strange Gardener' is a linocut from his schooldays. The rest are line drawings for the volume, *Bête Noire,* which he was preparing just before his death. They are now reproduced for the first time. Many other drawings and paintings, as well as the manuscripts of almost fifty poems, are in the British Museum.

We cannot let this occasion pass without expressing our admiration for the courageous devotion Mrs. Douglas gave her son during his life, and our gratitude for the help she has unhesitatingly given us in our editorial task.

JOHN WALLER
G. S. FRASER
J. C. HALL

INTRODUCTION

To my constant regret my impressions of Keith Douglas are almost confined to that sad and wild time when the second World War was imminent and when it was actual, though I did not see much of him once he had begun his special training and duly taken his commission. At least I had the good fortune of meeting, in their health and strength, two of the chief poets whom that War did not allow to live on and exert their imaginative and personal powers on the world which has moved along such mysterious ways since 1945. The other, Sidney Keyes, I knew but little. With Keith Douglas naturally, our background being the same ancient school and ancient College at Oxford, my meetings were many and on many concerns; that is, in 1938 and 1939 particularly, between his schooldays and his going to the wars.

His school, as his editors duly note, was Christ's Hospital, and I had only to be with him for ten minutes—he came to me while I was the tutor in English Literature at Merton College—in order to know his two predominant loyalties. One was to his mother, the other to the Bluecoat School. Keith had the advantage of being well befriended by one of his schoolmasters, the late D. S. Roberts, who wrote that 'with his death Christ's Hospital has lost one of her most gifted and vivid personalities.' It is typical of his feeling for his old school that in his war journal, *Alamein to Zem Zem*, Douglas returns, right in the crash of battle, to Christ's Hospital chapel and one of Frank Brangwyn's murals there for a comparison.

Keith was one of the most outspoken of people, as many accounts agree, but to his Tutor (capital T in those days) he was infallibly gentle and attentive. He took plenty of trouble over his weekly essay, even when his passion for horsemanship (and his friendship with the amusing Hamo Sassoon, another pupil of mine) preoccupied him. Handwriting—ever clear and flowing; but then, so was the expression. Brevity—but nothing impecunious about it. Substance—as matter-of-fact as he could make it! He did not care about novelty when he was finding his way.

Outside our tutorial sessions I remember one or two Oxford, typically Oxford schemes, in which he took pleasure and for which he worked as he could work once he accepted the cause. I proposed a miscellany of prose and verse to be entitled *Augury*, and Keith quickly joined his friend Alec Hardie in assembling it. It was eventually published by Messrs. Blackwell; and for the senior and junior members of the university who contributed to it, it had the purpose of recommending the humanities at a time when the inhumanities were gathering round.

Another engrossing scheme was a performance of Dryden's *Secular Mask*—on the ending of an old age and the beginning of a new. Now we realized, if we had not already done so, that Keith was deeply devoted to the stage; he assisted us in all the preparations for this operatic piece (a shame that there was no part for him to act), spending many hours unseen to us in attempting to supply papier-mâché masks. These were revealed and had merit, but unfortunately collapsed before they could be displayed to the audience. After the show Keith used all his art (and he was a painter always looking about for some opportunity, some untried nicety) on a decorated poem in honour of the cast and, if I may say it here, of the senior member who played Chronos with a beach-ball as the globe he was compelled to carry.

With Keith Douglas, indeed, poetry and painting were twin preoccupations. Another Mertonian, Douglas Grant, has ventured the opinion that Keith 'might have excelled eventually as the artist rather than as the poet.' It was to nature, especially to horses and their settings, that he first applied his art and his fresh bright colours. Later, he used the same painter's skill to depict the turmoil and 'nightmare ground' of the desert campaign.

Keith's character was, I believe, complex in the manner of many artists. Against his generosity and zest for life must be placed, if the portrait is to be (as he would have wished it to be) true to life, certain less endearing qualities—an impulsive and obstinate streak which was sometimes the despair of even his closest friends. His intellect was as I now feel on the verge of greatness. It is on this account that his poetry, and his poetry was not only the fruit of his war experiences, looks like answering the demand of his distant school predecessor Coleridge: the best poets utter a philosophy. Keith Douglas was (in the words of one of his schoolmasters) 'one of the ablest of our History Grecians', and had formed his panorama of life and time out of his historical contemplations. His mythology was energetic, for he had not noticed that the classical world had been sent to Coventry. He was a young man who often did not notice such things.

Introducing Douglas's *Selected Poems* in 1964, Mr. Ted Hughes gave the opinion that 'he offers more than just a few poems about war, and that every poem he wrote, whether about war or not, has some special value. His poetry in general seems to be of some special value. It is still very much alive, and even providing life. And the longer it lives, the fresher it looks'. It is good to find a poet of a later generation writing thus of Keith twenty years after his death. For myself, I will shelter behind the ample solidity of Samuel Johnson when in his short life of the poet William Collins he brought back what he had written on Collins in earlier years. The critical notice that follows is dated winter 1944, and the reader will easily adjust it in minor points to the present time; like Dr. Johnson in the case of Collins, I think it is clearer than what I might write now, notwithstanding all the fuller 'materials'.

'As the poems of Keith Douglas are as yet uncollected (though there is a volume in preparation), it is not easy to express a full opinion on them; but one especial characteristic is clear—they were the work of a painter-poet, and highly pictorial. His thoughts and fancies were curious, his emotions were not everybody's, and he strove to present these in sharp designs of image and allusion. His observation of the arts, no matter what the period or the place, was extremely keen, and provided him when he wrote verse with these figures and their strong colours. As yet, his topics were principally personal, yet his mind's eye saw in them the recurrence of experience of wider range and longer date than his own. We must grieve that it happened with him as with some young writers of the generation before, writers whom he honoured; it was war which brought him towards the maturity of his poetry. Some of his latest pieces are, I think, his best; the complexity which overlaid much that he meant has gone, and he is governed by the great argument of the time—that becomes the rhythm and the feeling of his lyrics. But still the singular touch of his pictorial sense signs the poems.

'He hated decoration without anything behind it, but his verse is decorative, and, thinking of it, I think of figureheads and lamias, or of the masks which he devised so eagerly; yet it was his real aim in pleasing the imagination thus to impress truths of human affairs which he came at in his independent way. He did not wish to startle with novelty, but to fashion his work as best suited his kind of thinking, whether that was unanticipated or after all of an ancient kind. The very look of his manuscripts is interesting as a help to understanding his poetic mood; they are written freely and gracefully, as though he saw his abstractions as definitely as physical objects. And this he maintained throughout his varied circumstances on active service'.

EDMUND BLUNDEN

SCHOOLDAYS

MUMMERS

Put by your stitching. Spread the table
With winking cups and wines. That sable
Doff for your brighter silks: are all
Your glints of pearly laughter shuttered?
See where the outdoor snows, wind-fluttered,
Through the arch window fall.

See where the deep night's blast has straddled
The ancient gargoyle, weather-addled
And striped with melted tapestry
Of snow; his evil face well-carven
By Brother Ambrose, lean and starven,
Cell-fasting, rich in artistry.

Soon come the masked mummers, knocking
With hands snow-red. The door's unlocking
Answers the stars with indoor light.
Now to the drum tap, with snow-crusted
Cardboard steed, and ancient rusted
Blade, the Saint and Turk will fight.

1934

Now my mind's off again. No tears
Of Catullus move me. Though I know, in turn
We too will praise these years
Of watching clouds through windows, fluttering pages,
Usefully sometimes, though the beckoning scents
Rise always, wafted from summer grass.
Hearing the loud bees mumble at the glass
And sound of sunlight behind the scratching pens,
We crouch to read the speech of other ages.

Many were here, some cursed, loved some. All these
Alike pass; after a space return,
Loud-voiced, mocking the older memories.

1935

FAMOUS MEN

And now no longer sung,
not mourning, not remembered
more under the sun,

not enough their deserved
praise. The quick movement of dactyls
does not compensate them.

The air is advertised of seas
they smote, from green to copper.
They were merciful men.

And think, like plates lie deep
licked clean their skulls,
rest beautifully, staring.

1935

CARAVAN

Going beyond the gate they found these men
Sitting in the last light and regarding the great sun
With understanding. And one spoke to them presently
Saying he had discovered the soul of music
At one time. And another said that when
The birds flew southwards, heading across the continent,

Then the attained sea, under the always rhythmic
Shutter of wingtips, only suggests to spent
Eyes slanting, the slope of green and mountainous moving
Country; familiar, only no priests in the cities
Handling the cold bronze, counting. The stones in panic
Chilled, the bright dust reflecting the heavens' faces.

Thus he revealed the perfect sources, the lost
Wisdom, seeing only the loved existent;
The clouds flying, Earth stretching in silence,
Chameleon, the colours limited, dyes all lost.
All this he told them, speaking the tongue of the swallows.

But they not knowing the words, nor in his hands
Seeing the meaning, went thence over the sands.

1935

IMAGES

The small men walk about antlike
and the bell tolls. God created these
beautiful and angular, not different.

The straight men are not there now
and their dark spears do not lean against the sun.
Not any more, since the bell has begun tolling.

The priests were acquainted with them,
making chips in the pyramids,
at intervals in the warm stone.

The bell will go on tolling
to kings on their marble bases.
But these are the unacknowledged rulers:

and understanding the bell they do not hear it,
but walk over the hilltop
into their rarer climate.

1935

YOUTH

Your sword is brilliant; through the auburn leaves
The sun patches your tunic of smooth-woven green,
Each fold a thousand aery shimmers cleaves
Dazzling as leaping fish a moment seen.

The road curls down below you. In its spell
Pass glebe and woodland, where a hundred ways
Twist, some to fairyland, and some to Hell;
But there are better things beyond the maze.

When you have heard the whirl and song of strife,
When use scratches and rusts your weapons' gleam
And age has marred the youngness of your life
With dreams, you will come back again, and dream.

1935

STRANGE GARDENER

Over the meadow,
framed in the quiet osiers, dreams the pond;
region of summer gnat-busyness
and, in the afternoon's blue drowsiness,
plops among the water-shadows:
and the cool trees wait beyond.

A young man dwelt there
with a swift, sad face, and full of phantasy,
repeating, as he heard it,
the alliterative speech of the water-spirit;
smoothing his pale hair
with automatic ecstasy.

This was his garden,
uncultivated (order hated him);
whence, in a winter-madness
(whose scourge filled him with recklessness,
seeing the frost harden),
the water-spirit translated him.

1935

I have looked through the pine-trees
Cooling their sun-warmed needles in the night,
I saw the moon's face white
    Beautiful as the breeze.

Yet you have seen the boughs sway with the night's breath,
Wave like dead arms, repudiating the stars
And the moon, circular and useless, pass
    Pock-marked with death.

Through a machine-gun's sights
I saw men curse, weep, cough, sprawl in their entrails;
You did not know the gardener in the vales,
    Only efficiency delights you.

1935

BEXHILL

And, now in the South, the swallows
Are not known, not at this season, among these
Small streets and posters which the lamplight shews:
But are among the white-dusted avenues,
And where the ruined palace faces the green
Isonzo, the barbers chatter, the sky is clean.

1935

ENCOUNTER WITH A GOD

Ono-no-komache the poetess
sat on the ground among her flowers,
sat in her delicate-patterned dress
thinking of the rowers,
thinking of the god Daikoku.

Thinking of the rock pool
and carp in the waterfall at night.
Daikoku in accordance with the rule
is beautiful, she said, with a slight
tendency to angles.

But Daikoku came
who had been drinking all night
with the greenish gods of chance and fame.
He was rotund standing in the moonlight,
with a round, white paunch.

Who said
I am not beautiful,
I do not wish to be wonderfully made,
I am not intoxicated, dutiful daughter,
and I will not be in a poem.

But the poetess sat still
holding her head and making verses:
'How intricate and peculiarly well-
arranged the symmetrical belly-purses
of Lord Daikoku.'

1936

33

DEJECTION

Yesterday travellers in summer's country,
Tonight the sprinkled moon and ravenous sky
Say, we have reached the boundary. The autumn clothes
Are on; Death is the season and we the living
Are hailed by the solitary to join their regiment,
To leave the sea and the horses and march away
Endlessly. The spheres speak with persuasive voices.

Only tomorrow like a seagull hovers and calls
Shrieks through the mist and scatters the pools of stars.
The windows will be open and hearts behind them.

1936

SONNET

Curtaining this country the whispering rain
Stipples in cold monochrome the sun's
Alive and tinted picture, so warm once;
The wind's voice laden like reeds with random pain.

Impending with their frown the bowed trees,
Clouds make a ceiling by the rooks' village
At which how vainly they complain, silly
Voices fall down, lost in the day's disease.

Like all, this storm will blunder along the hills,
Retire muttering into a smutty corner
Of sky, and there dying, his rant stills.

Wait. See like a tired giant the sun return
To step into your valley and gladly fill
Evening with moist colour, made untarnished.

1936

KRISTIN

This season like a child on airy points
Has crept behind you in an evening time
To take you unawares and touch your hair
With a gift of gold; or like a messenger
Arrives on the scene saying a god's wants,
To exile the dull colours and make us sublime.

Presently then our simple friend the sun
Will climb and watch out of his summer tower
To see us play this country interlude:
Love like the lovely plants he wants renewed—
Take it all back after the sun has gone
Perhaps, but humour him this candle hour.

Yes, futile to prolong this natural instant:
Black days lean over, hours curtailed with fear.
But look, bedewèd violets lip the rain,
A little forlorn magic has homed again.
Take this, these limpid days will not be constant;
They will forsake you, will not reappear.

1937

VILLANELLE OF GORIZIA

Over and over the street is repeated with sunlight,
the oxen tire even of the leaves,
the flutes sound in the wineshop out of sight.

The sky is apathetic like a kite
that cares not how the string below it weaves
over and over. The street is repeated with sunlight

till only doors are dark among the white
walls that outstare the sun. And noon achieves
the flutes' sound in the wineshop, out of sight.

The town cannot remember when was night,
the trees droop for the subtle-coloured eves,
over and over the street is repeated with sunlight.

The short shades of the avenues invite
the monk with his umbrella, who perceives
the flutes sound in the wineshop, out of sight.

All this the bottle says, that I have quite
poured out. The wine slides in my throat and grieves.
Over and over the street is repeated with sunlight,
the flutes sound in the wineshop, out of sight.

1937

POINT OF VIEW

Old man or young man, if you are like me, like
To trace the turkish shadow on the down,
The busybody engine in the distance—
In your mind's ear the horses like a pistol
Smack on the odd stone, rabble of winds at hill's crown
Egg them on. Or in the orchestra by the dyke

The chorus of reeds to talk when people have passed
Saying they're gone, they're gone, huddling like chums.
Yes, if this sort of thing is your middle name
Or if you are at home, sit and cry shame
To step at the dusk's edge with seductive summer,
Shut out the fields and search for facts too fast—

Whichever it is, whichever ambition expands
Across your horizon, or dream your soul enjoys;
If you are this, or if you wear that token,
Who'll say, when nurse has had her nap and woken,
Who is to tell, when she takes away our toys,
Which of us will catch tears in his simple hand?

1937

ON LEAVING SCHOOL

Here where the years stand under us in the valley
We can look down upon their shops and vineyards
And honestly say, we had rather be like leopards
Let loose in one direction, who cannot be silly.

This simple evening moment, when the shallow
Echoes stagger against Big School, it is awkward
Realizing happiness seems just to have started
And now we must leave it, live like trees or charlock.

One of us will be the kettle past care of tinkers,
Rejected, one the tip-top apple, the winking
Sun's friend. It will be that way, and Time on our ground

Will sweep like a maid, and where we were be clean.
Shall we find room to laugh, if turning round
We see where we have walked, how wrong we have been?

1937

OXFORD

FORGOTTEN THE RED LEAVES

Forgotten the red leaves painting the temple in summer,
Forgotten my squirrel in his dark chamber,
The great turtle and the catamaran;
Rivers, where the mosaic stones are found.

That church, amputated by high explosive,
Where priests no more lift up their murmurous Latin,
And only the sun, a solitary worshipper,
Tiptoes towards the altar and rests there.

These and the hazy tropic where I lived
In tall seas where the bright fish go like footmen
Down the blue corridors about their business,
The jewelled skulls are down there. I have forgot,

Almost forgot. How slowly they return
Like princes into the rooms they once owned. How dimly
I see the imaginary moon, the magic painter
Of long, deserted acres with splendour and silence.

Once on Monte Nero in the spring
Some peasant girl fashioned for love and work
Taught me a smile that I had forgotten,
It is so hard to speak her language now.

Almost forgot. How slowly they return
Like princes into the halls they once owned.

1938

STRANGER
(*For Y.C.S.*)

What in the pattern of your face
Was writing to my eye, that journeyed once
Like an explorer in your beauty's land,
To find that venerable secret stand
Somehow carved there; and ever since
Has rested still, enchanted by the place?

Cast up along your eyes' dark shore
There, or within the cool red cave of lips,
My heart would spend a solitary spell,
Delighted hermit in his royal cell.
For your eyes and your precious mouth perhaps
Are blessed isles once found and found no more.

You are the whole continent of love
For me, the windy sailor on this ocean,
Who'd lose his ragged vessel to the waves
And call on you, the strange land, to save.
Here I set up my altar and devotion,
And let no storm blot out the place I have.

1938

SPRING SAILOR

That high-decked cloud adventuring along
All day to anchor in the visionary
Night's land, has moved the birds in melody
Like harmless sirens to accompany
His silent voyage. Behold him now lie
Moored up beside the six trees, among

The islands of the sun, the distant isles.
And now the birds, the thriftless balladmongers,
Break off his tale and begin to tell
The marvellous story without words, and still
Beyond your speech. These many skilful singers
Easily start your silly tears and smiles.

I will contrive to escape the dainty touch
Of a day so heavy with the imagery
Of longing. And the various eyes of earth
Opening, the dreams ready for their rebirth,
Even the gentle hands of earth for me
Shall move without disquieting me much.

1939

POOR MARY

Death has made up your face, his quiet hand
Perfects your costume to impersonate
The one who cannot enter this living land.

And it is death who makes sure, and chances
No tenderness in the recesses of your eyes.
In the halls of your heart no spirit dances,

But you are the house of sorrow. In you all
Colours are dark and casemented for ever,
No answering song inside the cold wall.

For to the travellers who cry, Death
Come out and say why you are living there,
He will not answer; they have lost their breath.

Only an effigy bobbing at the pane
Cries out with starling speech and falls down,
And there is silence in the house again.

1939

INVADERS

Intelligences like black birds
come on their dire wings from Europe. Sorrows
fall like the rooks' clatter on house and garden.
And who will drive them back before we harden?
You will find, after a few tomorrows
like this, nothing will matter but the black birds.

You will not paint lips on your lips
or beautify yourself in anyone's eyes:
I shall never write a word to escape,
our life will take on a hard shape;
and then if we are spared we shall not arise
to hold the world up when it finally slips.

So keep a highlight in your handsome eye;
still be fastidious, and I will write
some well-intentioned words. We with our heart
still sensitive as air will do our part,
always to think, and always to indite
of a good matter, while the black birds cry.

1939

PAS DE TROIS

Three dancers under music's orders stand
held by the hand of silence for a moment
posing. Now somewhere the flutes' sound
lifts the enchantment. Easily unbound,
they begin to move like plants and nod slowly
their three heads like blooms; their tendril hands

describe the shapes of air. Behold their feet
on points of strength such as grass has,
gently to divide the strength of stone,
make them like gods miraculously borne:
Sonia, Tania, Katia, strange deities,
who sign to us and whom we may not greet.

Theirs is a craft of quiet:
they are shades of an old time
when you could hear, no riot
intervening, intricate and frail rhyme
and music; men had leisure
to ornament, only for pure pleasure,
their utensils and their life;
to live an hour or make a knife
intent on every jewelled space.

Today when smartness does for grace,
this is why they interlace
their precious hands and dance their pace
of three before your ordinary face.

1939

Music creates two grenadiers, scarlet and tall
Leisurely fellows: in the long afternoon
They stroll with royal slow motion. How they twirl
Their regular canes. Each silly servant girl
Regards wide-eyed or diffidently, soon
Is captured quite. The idle lords of all

The park, the dogs, the children, both wheel
Down the long walk between the lazy trees.
Yet scrutinize the regimental pair
And you will find, they are but men of air—
Their summer is a fantasy, and these
Like all authenic heroes are unreal.

Follow them none the less at the same pace:
For you perhaps to step behind these two
May shew such dead romances can revive,
The painted blackcloth quicken and be alive.
You will look out upon this painted view
Of madmen in a non-existent place.

1939

HAYDN—CLOCK SYMPHONY

The timepiece standing butler in the hall
Beneath the remote ceiling, with the same
Grave air as Time himself, will let you pass
To quiz your elegant person in a glass
And enter the long room. The brilliant game
Of dancing's at its height, the panic fall

And rise of music on the amazing floor
Where dresses, white dresses, sweep and dip
To the high notes as distant as the moon.
By a polite enchantment of the tune
Detained, step opposite some cherry lip,
Dark eye and oval countenance demure.

Consider, Sir, you move in eternity here:
No wonder you have the carriage of a god,
For here you are the man who in your sleep
Walks in the corridors and in the deep
Recesses of your mind; where you have trod
The polished ground of dreaming every year.

Yet you Death's servant must return to service:
Re-enter the hall and find the solemn clock
Who cries that Time's alive. And so put on
Your garment of sad days and get you gone.
Against you and your raucous world they'll lock,
But open up when you forsake Death's service.

1939

VILLANELLE OF SUNLIGHT

The sunlight settled on a wall
Magical traveller through the air,
Fills my heart with funerall

For all the dead who were the tall
Lovers and beauties, who found here
The sunlight settled on a wall.

They who were richest, they recall
None of their treasures. So despair
Fills my heart. With funerall

And with no usual mirth let fall
A sign of sorrow. Even fear
The sunlight settled on a wall.

For fear, that some which heard his call
Now are cold and do not care,
Fills my heart with funerall.

This sunlight, sojourner for all
These centuries, maintains his stare.
O, sunlight settled on a wall
Fills my heart with funerall.

1940

STARS

(*For Antoinette*)

The stars still marching in extended order
Move out of nowhere into nowhere. Look, they are halted
On a vast field tonight, true no man's land.
Far down the sky with sword and belt must stand
Orion. For commissariat of this exalted
War-company, the Wain. No fabulous border

Could swallow all this bravery. No band
Will ever face them: nothing but discipline
Has mobilized and still maintains them. Thus
Time and his ancestors have seen them. Thus
Always to fight disorder is their business,
And victory continues in their hand.

From under the old hills to overhead
And down there marching on the hills again
Their camp extends. There go the messengers,
Comets, with greetings of ethereal officers
From tent to tent. Yes, we look up with pain
At distant comrades and plains we cannot tread.

LEUKOTHEA

When you were alive, my Leukothea,
your loveliness was puzzling
and only I knew the processes
by which my ornament lived and breathed.
And when you died
I was persuaded to store you in the earth
and I remember when they put you there
your too expressive living eye
being covered by the dark eyelash
and by its lid for a cerement.
At that moment those who looked at you
wondered I know how you could be made
in such exquisite material
and I would not explain for the world.
Even when they put the soil above you
they saw its unusual texture. The very grass
was a strange plant, precious as emeralds.

So all these years I have lived securely. I knew
I had only to uncover you
to see how the careful earth would have kept
all as it was, untouched. I trusted the ground.
I knew the worm and the beetle would go by
and never dare batten on your beauty.

Last night I dreamed and found my trust betrayed
only the little bones and the great bones disarrayed.

1940

SHADOWS

Shadows are waters: in these forgetful caves
they stand or flow, purple and rich
on the rich earth. A dim tunnel of trees
wards off the whirling men and deities
from these involved corridors; that stretch
where memory easily makes graves

for dead sorrows, and has herself not long
to exist. Only thought swims about.
The sunlight filtering through leaves like glass
with flame putrified will even pass
into the darkest channel of the moat.
But to the somnolent earth falls no song

or sound. It is sacrilege of course to speak,
but I am here for silence: I had heard
the property of the place to heal,
and have come here not to feel
a wound winter and summer have not deterred
from aching. And I find this charm as weak.

1940

ABSENCE

The long curtained French windows conceal
the company at dinner by candlelight.
I am the solitary person on the lawn,
dressed up silver by the moon.
The bush on my left sleeps, the tree on my right
is awake but stays motionless to feel,

as I and Cupid on his ornament stone,
how the whole evening here discourses
and the stars too lean nearer to the earth
for their traditional splendour pours forth
much more in such unpopulous places,
almost litters the trees like rain.

So the minutes assemble at first in silence
till here or there the speech of ghosts or leaves
is audible. And it appears each grieves,
the garden with its composite voice sighing:
She is not here and you who come instead
shew by your attitude she's dead.

1940

THE POETS

Once merchants, when the impassive sands
stare us out, and the sun, we long for towns—
but as we enter, the dealers spread their hands

in a gesture which means I have not,
not for you; mock us with obscenities or frowns.
In these settlements nothing, nothing is got

by strangers; nothing is accepted.
When we speak, even our words are bad
currency, to which they take exception.

And here, in squalid content
an ancient people lives. Is it not sad,
in a decade or two they'll be extinct.

But we ourselves are already phantoms;
boneless, substanceless, wanderers; they look at us
with primitive mistrust. Not even the wantons

roll eyes in our direction. For we are hated,
known to be cursed, guessed to be venomous;
we must advance for ever, always belated.

1940

THE CREATOR

The unwearied sun from day to day
along his mathematic way
looks with an infant's eyes upon
what little in the world's not wrong;
and with no understanding tear
at the death of a sad year.

So he forgets and turns away west,
while with fine uninterest
and in bone idle groups the stars
stupidly linger, and watch pass
erupting woe and queasy mirth
across the sallow face of earth.

And surely God, with never less
ignorance of pity or remorse,
is gaping at the eternal course
of sorrow, all His planning. Yes,
He's petrified and cannot see
His marvellous inefficiency.

1940

VILLANELLE OF SPRING BELLS

Bells in the town alight with spring
converse, with sweet concordance of new airs
make clear the fresh and aged sound they sing.

People emerge from winter to hear them ring,
children glitter with mischief and the blind man hears
bells in the town alight with spring.

Even he on his eyes feels the caressing
finger of Persephone, and her voice escaped from tears
makes clear the fresh and aged sound they sing.

Bird feels the enchantment of his wing
and in ten fine notes dispels twenty cares.
Bells in the town alight with spring

warble the praise of Time, for he can bring
this season: chimes the merry welkin bears
make clear the fresh and aged sound they sing.

All evil men intent on evil thing
falter, for in their cold unready ears
bells in the town alight with spring
make clear the fresh and aged sound they sing.

1940

SANCTUARY

Once my mother was a wall;
behind my rampart and my keep
in a safe and hungry house
I lay as snug as winter mouse:
till the wall breaks and I weep
for simple reasons first of all.

All the barriers give in,
the world will lance at every point
my unsteady heart, still and still
to subjugate my tired will.
When it's done they will anoint me
being kinder if they win.

So beyond a desperate fence
I'll cross where I shall not return,
the line between indifference
and my vulnerable mind:
no more then kind or unkind
touch me, no love nor hate burn.

1940

A ROUND NUMBER

The monotonous evil clock
is creeper climbing on my heart
and with rank ivy will pull down
my hope of happiness and renown.

My sacred lady who needs no art
gives an idiot place to mock.

I know the fragrant girl is dead,
and perished with my innocence
and died two hundred years ago:
or twice that time if Time is slow.

And so reflect for recompense
she only lived inside my head.

Then she is gone. I still remember
my early promise, looking for

obliging fame to make amends,
and here my last existence ends.

For I can't feel hope any more
and Time has reached a round number.

SEARCH FOR A GOD

Turn away from Monte Nero, that mountain
to the west. Turn your back on the white town
of Gorizia, plastered with notices and swarming
with soldiers. Cross the green Isonzo: go down

by the ruined palace of the archbishop, the machine-gun schools,
and a company of the Alpini with their mules.
Now uphill to the woods where hundreds of saplings hide
where a generation of men and trees died.

And where the bright blood and shrapnel are sunk in grass
the golden oriole fluting in a cool hollow
colours the silence. These musical spirits pass
ahead and to the left. Now if you follow

you will come where high explosive could not move
the god interred beneath this flowering grove,
but he has slept two hundred decades here.

No music will wake his marble: not yet,
still he must lie in soil and forget
another madness begun this year.

SOISSONS

(*For Hamo Sassoon*)

M. l'Epicier in his white hat
in an outhouse by the cathedral, makes
devils from the selfsame stone
men used in the religious century.
The cathedral itself in new masonry
stands openly in this sunlit town
of Soissons. Down the long hill snakes
the hard hot road into the town's heart.

In the evening when the late sunlight abandons
buildings still glimmering from shadow on shadow
someone leans from the window eavesdropping our
strange voices so late in the cathedral square.
From the barracks of the 19th Regiment you can hear
the equivalent of Lights Out. Now the sweet-sour
wine clambers in our heads. Go in. Tomorrow
tiptoes with us along the dark landing.

'A Laon, belle Cathédrale,' making
a wave of his white hat, explains
the maker of gargoyles. So we take
a route for Laon and Rheims leaving you
Soissons, a simplified mediaeval view
taken from a Book of Hours. How dark
seems the whole country we enter. Now it rains,
and trees like ominous old men are shaking.

1940

This town is no tower of the mind
and the cathedral, not an edifice of air, stands
dignified and sleepy with serenity—
so I would have said, and that this solid city
was built here close under the angels' hands,
something we had no longer reckoned to find.

Yet here something of the mind lived and died,
a mental tower restored only to fall
and we in England heard it come down
as though of all, this was the most ominous sound.
The devils pilloried in that holy wall
must smile to see our faith broke to the wide.

You who believe you have a kind creator
are with your sire crowding into twilight,
as using excellent smooth instruments
material man makes himself immense.
Oh you may try, but can't deny he's right
and what he does and destroys makes him greater.

1940

EXTENSION TO FRANCIS THOMPSON

Look in earth and air to catch
his mineral or electric eye.
And in the universe his voice
assumes perfect diversity.

The natural laws his angels are
and circumspectly go about
leaving marks the learned know
one for man to follow out.

Leo in drawing Deirdre's lips
drew as hand and pen were sent
by heaven. This perfection slips
through the hand to the instrument.

Expert diplomats' good taste
the curious statement of a child
or in his enamelled case
the doughty beetle hard and wild.

All in different degrees
embody the celestial thing
and the wise man will learn of these
analysis is worshipping.

1940

THE DECEASED

He was a reprobate I grant
and always liquored till his money went.

His hair depended in a noose from
a Corona Veneris. His eyes, dumb

like prisoners in their cavernous slots, were
settled in attitudes of despair.

You who God bless you never sunk so low
censure and pray for him that he was so;

and with his failings you regret the verses
the fellow made, probably between curses,

probably in the extremes of moral decay,
but he wrote them in a sincere way:

and appears to have felt a refined pain
to which your virtue cannot attain.

Respect him. For in this
he had an excellence you miss.

1940

REPROACH

You're handsome and false, and I could cover
that face with praise till I've stretched over
a figurative mask of words
for beauty; or my pen unloads
all that's packed up in the mind.
Then call a truce, and never find
enough, you are so fair, to do you honour.

The only voice to put with yours
Ulysses heard and strained the hawse
till it scarce held him to the sane mast—
I think your hair so glistened last
when Troilus found you in your uncle's hall,
jettisoned his arms with a humble gesture, fell
conquered, poor hero, in a deceitful house.

And if to portray you will exhaust
legends, illusion, eloquence, what most
will abash all my ingenuity
is doing justice to your perfidy.
Cressida could not match you, but I pray
you'll feel Cressida's ruin and decay
who was known for a strumpet, and outcast.

1940

RUSSIANS

How silly that soldier is pointing his gun at the wood:
he doesn't know it isn't any good.
You see, the cold and cruel northern wind
has frozen the whole battalion where they stand.

That's never a corporal: even now he's frozen
you could see he's only a commercial artist
whom they took and put those clothes on,
and told him he was one of the smartest.

Russians

Even now they're in ice it's easy to know
what a shock it was, a long shock
that's been coming home to them wherever they go,
with their mazy minds taking stock.

Walk among the innocuous parade
and touch them if you like, they're properly stayed:
keep out of their line of sight and they won't look.
Think of them as waxworks, or think they're struck

with a dumb immobile spell,
to wake in a thousand years with the sweet force
of spring upon them in the merry world. Well,
at least forget what happens when it thaws.

1940

A MIME

Time and Death, villains in the wings,
stretch out their fingers parallel
at me. Death says: 'If I don't get you,
then Time aha will presently upset you—
you'll find how soon his famous spell
will coil you in successive strings.'

'But Sir,' says he, old melodramatic Death,
'May I be the first one after all,
and Time young man will spare you, for
the young fill my fastidious maw
more tastily. Revel and grow tall,
and rest you merry near your last breath.'

In deference to his advice
I look in maidens' faces after
what men cannot but need the most.
But Time as limber as a ghost
dispelling kisses and sweet laughter
looks to catch me in a trice.

Only between these dangerous two
let me be nimble, jump and dodge
the unnatural uncles on my track;
if I don't croak and falter back
despairing in the end to cadge
careless hearts from you and you.

1940

JOHN ANDERSON

John Anderson, a scholarly gentleman
advancing with his company in the attack
received some bullets through him as he ran.

So his creative brain whirled, and he fell back
in the bloody dust (it was a fine day there
and warm). Blood turned his tunic black

while past his desperate final stare
the other simple soldiers run
and leave the hero unaware.

Apt epitaph or pun
he could not hit upon, to grace
a scholar's death; he only eyed the sun.

But I think, the last moment of his gaze
beheld the father of gods and men,
Zeus, leaning from heaven as he dies,

whom in his swoon he hears again
summon Apollo in the Homeric tongue:
Descend Phoebus and cleanse the stain

of dark blood from the body of John Anderson.
Give him to Death and Sleep,
who'll bear him as they can

out of the range of darts to the broad vale
of Lycia; there lay him in a deep
solemn content on some bright dale.

And the brothers, Sleep and Death
lift up John Anderson at his last breath.

1940

GENDER RHYME

A man, a name of people, and a wind;
river and mountain feel them complete
a mile or two to cavernous oblivion.

Man the little giant and the sweet
bully hero has burst his entrails to defend
a people that's dead now. So the trivial

wind blows over the hero and his kind
over river and mountain to limbo in the end.

1940

A BALLET

How cleverly the choreographer
and costumier combine—
the effect's fine and the young lady's line
impeccable. With what grace her arabesque
he caps with an entrechat, this tastefully dressed
young person, her partner.

All the colours of spring
they are dressed in;
they whirl about
and, the dance over, they gracefully leap out.

But here they come again, I'm certain, or
is this not the fair
young sylph? I declare
she has a dead face and a yellow eye
and he has no limbs—how dreadfully spry
he is on his stumps;
he bleeds, but he jumps
ten feet at a prance.
I don't like this dance.

1940

CANOE

Well, I am thinking this may be my last
summer, but cannot lose even a part
of pleasure in the old-fashioned art of
idleness. I cannot stand aghast

at whatever doom hovers in the background;
while grass and buildings and the somnolent river,
who know they are allowed to last for ever,
exchange between them the whole subdued sound

of this hot time. What sudden fearful fate
can deter my shade wandering next year
from a return? Whistle and I will hear
and come another evening, when this boat

travels with you alone towards Iffley:
as you lie looking up for thunder again,
this cool touch does not betoken rain;
it is my spirit that kisses your mouth lightly.

1940

AN EXERCISE AGAINST IMPATIENCE

This city experiences a difficult time. The old bells
fall silent, or are bidden to silence. The buildings lean
inwards, watching the questionable sky,
and across the meadows, where youth and age inhabit,
exchange an austere opinion of foreboding.

This tremor must be sensible even to ghosts
of whom there are many here and there, travelling
carefully to and fro. They also question
perhaps, gesturing with their paper hands.

But all these whom wisdom and no curse keeps
in a kind of existence beyond their ordinary time here;
they must know how thought still works,
a hidden creator like the silkworm. It is this
to which I cling, and think will save us all.

For does not the tree stand, the broad hill
scarred by no worse wounds than before
he could sustain
and can easily resist again?
The colossal ocean on his crusty floor
is ordered by his influences still
and all the lights with mild simplicity shine
and clouds and atmosphere are the same
as they have been;
the seven winds, serene
or blusterous, as their nature is wild or tame
move from their quarters and return again.
And, in this circle caught,
spirits of every gentle sort
are in the heart
of every element, its richest part,
imprisoned; for at present taught
to abide motionless, they await their round.

Meanwhile these signs are not of the world's end,
it is another famous age they portend.

The work will be
for us now, only to wait:
then in the chaotic state
tomorrow, we can set these spirits free.

Even, we will command and wield
good forces. And if we die? And if we die
those we have met or heard of will not be cold,
they are as suitable as you or I.

And without prophets, what is there
in the crucible, the inscrutable cavern,
and what all the signs have given,
you can be certain, will appear.

1940

FAREWELL POEM

Please, on a day falling in summer,
recall how being tired, you and I
among the idle branches by the river
and blind to propriety and passers-by,
where leaves like eyes turn sidelong to the river,
fell asleep embraced and let the shades run
half crossing us, and half the vigorous sun,
till he had almost climbed enough.

Because tired, what innocents we were
protected by sleep you see we had not thought,
like a footprint before we were aware,
that day was complete behind us and wiped out:
so watch us broken apart and not aware,
keep prisoner pain and talk wry stuff.

Who is it that is pleased now we are sad,
who is satisfied and thanks his stars,
has got and has the happiness we had?
Will he enjoy long, or will the sudden alas,
and sorrow the light-fingered fellow pick his heart?
Of course: soon his misery will start,
for all delight is God's impermanent bluff.

In a minute he will come from the gold cloud,
the great black figure with a hideous laugh,
and hear the comfortable cry aloud:
the ethereal veil is cracked painted lath,
and he will be backed with fires and the red cloud.

We must never touch and start our story again;
for God is waiting with unexpended pain
and will not bless you my dark afflicted love.

1940

76

AN ORATION

In this city, lovers, beneath this moon,
greater here than elsewhere and more beautiful,
who loves conspiracies and lovers, here you walked.
It was you who spoke in the dark streets, stood in the shadows
or where the lamps lit your white faces and red lips.
Yours were the figures which moved and disappeared
by the great dark church and the taciturn river:
many spirits stood there with you,
stood beside you and embraced, shadow with shadow,
when you kissed. Even the poor dead
who in despair entered the water at night
were there. They also acquiesced when you said:
this is our town because of what we experienced here.

Here the hucksters cried their swindles and bargains,
clothes, scent, and finery of all kinds,
and here the balladmongers made their songs;
many songs were composed, truth was recited,
the perfect utterance of several ages.

But it is no longer the jewel and setting for jewels,
the ancient town in whose streets walked
centuries ago the saints and national heroes,
where the divines taught, and the populace
dragged up great stones to build the white churches.
Then it was a golden age. With what sincerity
even those who were wrong lived. The beggars were proud
to be the beggars of this noble town.

Even then the foreigners came to learn, to admire,
and in a time which some still remember
this was the city of amorists, collectors, and wits,
those among men to whom good things are given.
Consider then what sweet words and inventions
they spoke and thought; and yet, though some still live
who knew these, the people themselves are dead,
wakeful and miserable in their dark graves.

Yes, the dead are wakeful and swift, at once to know
when disgrace comes, strangers on their graves.
Meanwhile the living sleep like hogs
and in their sleep many strangers arrive
and they pathetically oblivious stand
imagining they are dreams; I cannot say
what they imagine, vain, impotent men.

But it is not irreparable. The city
may still stir, the lovely soul become
alive, alive, and all her beauty alive;
the fountains playing in the squares, the white buildings
standing erect, smiling on the day,
and all the pleasant traffic moving again.
Songs will appear like flowers, they'll sing and sing
and everywhere as it used to be, permanent spring
for which this town was known, will fly and dance
on the soft air, the food and wine flow
from all the fertile outskirts, plenty, plenty
for the poor and the rich, plenty for the admirers,
the visitors and those travelling through.
Such will the city be when she awakes.

This is not highflown language or impossibility
but the happy people I paint for you, today,
who are yourselves unhappy, you yourselves.
You are the happy people, when you unswoon,
poor marionettes, when you become real.

1940

ARMY: ENGLAND

THE PRISONER

Today, Cheng, I touched your face
with two fingers, as a gesture of love;
for I can never prove enough
by sight or sense your strange grace,

but mothwise my hands return
to your fair cheek, as luminous
as a lamp in a paper house,
and touch, to teach love and learn.

I think a hundred hours are gone
that so, like gods, we'd occupy.
But alas, Cheng, I cannot tell why,
today I touched a mask stretched on the stone

person of death. There was the urge
to break the bright flesh and emerge
of the ambitious cruel bone.

Royal Military College, Sandhurst, 1940

THE NEWS FROM EARTH

The limber monsters of the deep
quickening from an age of sleep
move in their dim viridian country
and soon, soon many a masthead sentry
will view Leviathan, like a continent, keep

the horizon to the North:
South all the humane porpoises dance forth,
sea nymphs and mermaidens with every scale
jewelled from the depth, lead on the ponderous whale
with musical and watery mirth.

And every luxurious beast with purple eye
in the hot East you shall espy
his second ornamental age begin.
See with alchemic horn and golden skin.
the heraldic Unicorn at leisure lie.

Sweet Zephyr also swims
down the soft air to meet his comrades. Pan begins
to address his pipe, unused to sing for years
and every hydrant deity uprears
with merry sound of splash his weedy limbs.

Out of the constellations all the Gods
leap down upon the mountains' cloudy heads
and all the unbending hills smile when
Bacchus at last conveys the news to men
and Cupid again leads lusty youth to bed.

Yes, Jove shouted once, and the whole illusion
chromium and machinery fell in fine confusion
vanished like a trick with all who lived by it;
yet none of us could wonder at the sight
of what might seem a wonderful conclusion.

Army Equitation School, Weedon, 1940

THE HOUSE

I am a pillar of this house
of which it seems the whole is glass
likewise transparent to the touch
for men like weightless shadows march
ignorantly in at the bright portico
or through a wall serenely go
unnoticing: myself am like a mouse
and carefully inspect all those that pass.

I am the pillar about which
like a conjured spectacle, such
amazing walls and floors appeared
as in the house that devils made.
Yet this queer magnificence
does not appear to many, its defence
not being walls but in the property
that it is thin as air and hard to see.

I am the pillar and again the one
walking a perpetual up-and-down
scrutinizing all these
substances, shadows on their ways
crowding or evacuating the place.
At times a voice singing, or a face
may seem suspended in the cunning air;
a voice by itself, a face traversing the stair
alone, like a mask of narrow porcelain.
These I introduce but lose again
which are of the imagination, or of air,
being in relation to the house, actually there
yet half illusion till I meet with one
who has that curious creative stone
to turn alive, to turn all alive:
prospecting this is all the care I have.

In order of appearance chosen by chance
whether it may have been to sing, to play, or to dance
to my mute invisible audience
many have performed here and gone hence.
Some have resided in the house for some time
the best rooms were theirs, also for them
scents and decorations were introduced
and other visitors were refused.
But when for months no man came near
an obscure feeling of suspicion and even fear
prompted me to climb and inspect the high
attic, where I made a disturbing discovery.
In this room which I had not entered for months
among the old pictures and bowls for hyacinths
and other refuse, I discovered the body
conventionally arranged, of a young lady
whom I admit I knew once, but had heard
declined in another country and there died.

Here's the strange fact, for here she lies.
If I but raise them my incredulous eyes
discern her, fairer now than when she lived
because on death her obscure beauty thrived;
the eyes turned to fine stones, the hair to flexible
gold, pale flesh to the most natural marble,
until she's the most permanent thing
in this impermanent building
and to remove her I must use
some supernatural device
it seems: for I am forced to say
she came here in a remarkable way.

I never studied such things; it will need a wiser
practitioner than me to exorcize her
but till the jewelled heart is dust and the gold head
disintegrates, I shall never hear the tread
of the visitor at whom I cannot guess,
the beautiful stranger, the princess.

Wickwar, Glos., 1941

OXFORD

At home, as in no other city, here
summer holds her breath in a dark street
the trees nocturnally scented, lovers like moths
go by silently on the footpaths
and spirits of the young wait,
cannot be expelled, multiply each year.

In the meadows, walks, over the walls
the sunlight, far-travelled, tired and content,
warms the recollections of old men, touching
the hand of the scholar on his book, marching
through quadrangles and arches, at last spent
it leans through the stained windows and falls.

This then is the city of young men, of beginning,
ideas, trials, pardonable follies,
the lightness, seriousness and sorrow of youth.
And the city of the old, looking for truth,
browsing for years, the mind's seven bellies
filled, become legendary figures, seeming

stones of the city, her venerable towers;
dignified, clothed by erudition and time.
For them it is not a city but an existence
outside which everthing is a pretence:
within, the leisurely immortals dream
venerated and spared by the ominous hours.

1941

TIME EATING

Ravenous Time has flowers for his food
in Autumn, yet can cleverly make good
each petal: devours animals and men,
but for ten dead he can create ten.

If you enquire how secretly you've come
to mansize from the smallness of a stone
it will appear his effort made you rise
so gradually to your proper size.

But as he makes he eats; the very part
where he began, even the elusive heart,
Time's ruminative tongue will wash
and slow juice masticate all flesh.

That volatile huge intestine holds
material and abstract in its folds:
thought and ambition melt and even the world
will alter, in that catholic belly curled.

But Time, who ate my love, you cannot make
such another; you who can remake
the lizard's tail and the bright snakeskin
cannot, cannot. That you gobbled in
too quick, and though you brought me from a boy
you can make no more of me, only destroy.

Wickwar, Glos., 1941

THE MARVEL

A baron of the sea, the great tropic
swordfish, spreadeagled on the thirsty deck
where sailors killed him, in the bright Pacific,

yielded to the sharp enquiring blade
the eye which guided him and found his prey
in the dim place where he was lord.

Which is an instrument forged in semi-darkness;
yet taken from the corpse of this strong traveller
becomes a powerful enlarging glass

reflecting the unusual sun's heat.
With it a sailor writes on the hot wood
the name of a harlot in his last port.

For it is one most curious device
of many, kept by the interesting waves,
for I suppose the querulous soft voice

of mariners who rotted into ghosts
digested by the gluttonous tides
could recount many. Let them be your hosts

and take you where their forgotten ships lie
with fishes going over the tall masts—
all this emerges from the burning eye.

And to engrave that word the sun goes through
with the power of the sea
writing her name and a marvel too.

Linney Head, Wales, 1941

SONG

Dotards do not think
but slowly slowly turn
eyes that have seen too much
and look for the soft touch
of Fate who cannot burn
but is a last drink,
a night drink, an opiate,
and almost comes too late.

I who could feel pain
a month, a month ago
and pleasure for my mind
and other pleasure find
like any dotard now
am wearily sat down,
a dull man, prisoner
in a dull chamber.

You who richly live
look at me, look at me;
stirred to talk with you
I say a word or two
like an effigy.
What answer will you give?
Will it wake the drugged man,
I wonder if you can.

White Horse Inn, Wickwar, Glos., 1941

SIMPLIFY ME WHEN I'M DEAD

Remember me when I am dead
and simplify me when I'm dead.

As the processes of earth
strip off the colour and the skin:
take the brown hair and blue eye

and leave me simpler than at birth,
when hairless I came howling in
as the moon entered the cold sky.

Of my skeleton perhaps,
so stripped, a learned man will say
'He was of such a type and intelligence,' no more.

Thus when in a year collapse
particular memories, you may
deduce, from the long pain I bore

the opinions I held, who was my foe
and what I left, even my appearance
but incidents will be no guide.

Time's wrong-way telescope will show
a minute man ten years hence
and by distance simplified.

Through that lens see if I seem
substance or nothing: of the world
deserving mention or charitable oblivion,

not by momentary spleen
or love into decision hurled,
leisurely arrive at an opinion.

Remember me when I am dead
and simplify me when I'm dead.

THE MIDDLE EAST

NEGATIVE INFORMATION

As lines, the unrelated symbols of
nothing you know, discovered in the clouds,
idly made on paper or by the feet of crowds
on sand, keep whatever meaning they have,

and you believe they write, for some
intelligence, messages of a sort—
these curious indentations on my thought
with every week, almost with each hour, come.

Perhaps you remember the fantastic moon
in the Atlantic—we descried the prisoner laden
with the thornbrush and the lantern—
the phosphorescence, the ship singing a sea-tune.

How we lost our circumstances that night
and like spirits attendant on the ship
now at the mast, now on the waves, might almost dip
and soar as lightly as our entranced sight.

Against that, the girls who met us at one place
were not whores, but women old and young at once
whom accidents turned to pretty stones,
to images slight with deceptive grace.

And in general, the account of many deaths—
whose portents, which should have undone the sky,
had never come—is now received casually.
You and I are careless of these millions of wraiths

for as often as not we meet
in dreams our own dishevelled ghosts;
and opposite, the modest hosts
of our ambition stare them out.

To this there's no sum I can find—
the hungry omens of calamity
mixed with good signs and all received with levity
or indifference by the amazed mind.

Palestine, November, 1941

SYRIA I

The grasses, ancient enemies
waiting at the edge of towns
conceal a movement of live stones,
the lizards with hooded eyes
of hostile miraculous age.

It is not snow on the green space
of hilltops, only towns of white
whose trees are populous with fruit
and girls whose velvet beauty is
handed down to them, gentle ornaments.

Here I am a stranger clothed
in the separative glass cloak
of strangeness. The dark eyes, the bright-mouthed
smiles, glance on the glass and break
falling like fine strange insects.

But from the grass, the inexorable lizard,
the dart of hatred for all strangers finds
in this armour, proof only against friends
breach after breach, and like the gnat is busy
wounding the skin, leaving poison there.

1941

These grasses, ancient enemies
waiting at the edge of towns,
conceal a movement of live stones,
the lizards with hooded eyes
of hostile miraculous age.

It is not snow on the green spurs
of hilltops, only towns of white
whose trees are populous with fruit;
with girls whose velvet beauty is
handed down to them, gentle ornaments.

Syria

Somewhere in the hard land
and vicious scrub, or fertile place
of women and productive trees
you think you see a devil stand
fronting a creature of good intention

or fair apples where the snake plays—
don't you? Sweet leaves but poisonous,
or a mantrap in a gay house,
a murderer with a lover's face
seem to you the signs of this country?

But devil and angel do not fight,
they are the classic Gemini
for whom it's vital to agree
whose interdependent state
this two-faced country reflects. Curiously

though foreigners we surely shall
prove this background's complement,
the kindly visitors who meant
so well all winter but at last fell
unaccountably to killing in the spring.

THE HAND

The hand is perfect in itself—the five
fingers, though changing attitude, depend
on a golden point, the imaginary true focal
to which infinities of motion and shape are yoked.
There is no beginning to the hand, no end,
and the bone retains its proportion in the grave.

I can transmute this hand, changing each
finger to man or a woman, and the hills
behind, drawn in their relation:
and to more than men, women, hills, by alteration
of symbols standing for the fingers, for the whole hand,
this alchemy is not difficult to teach,

this making a set of pictures, this drawing
shapes within the shapes of the hand—
an ordinary translation of forms. But hence
try to impose arguments
whose phases, each upon a digit, tend
to the centre of reasoning, the mainspring.

To do this is drilling the mind, still a recruit
for the active expeditions of his duty
when he must navigate alone the wild
cosmos, as the Jew wanders the world:
and we, watching the tracks of him at liberty
like the geometry of feet
upon a shore, constructed in the sand
look for the proportions, the form of an immense hand.

Nathanya, Palestine, 1941

THE SEA BIRD

Walking along beside the beach
where the Mediterranean turns in sleep
under the cliff's demiarch

through a curtain of thought I see
a dead bird and a live bird
the dead eyeless, but with a bright eye

the live bird discovered me
and stepped from a black rock into the air—
I turn from the dead bird to watch him fly,

electric, brilliant blue,
beneath he is orange, like flame,
colours I can't believe are so,

as legendary flowers bloom
incendiary in tint, so swift he
searches about the sky for room,

towering like the cliffs of this coast
with his stiletto wing
and orange on his breast:

he has consumed and drained
the colours of the sea
and the yellow of this tidal ground

till he escapes the eye, or is a ghost
and in a moment has come down
crept into the dead bird, ceased to exist.

Nathanya, Palestine, 1942

ADAMS

Walking beside the beach
where the Mediterranean turns in sleep
under the cliff's demiarch,

walking thinking slowly I see
a dead bird and live bird,
the dead eyeless: but with a bright eye

the live bird discovered me
stepping from a black rock into the air.
Leave the dead bird lie; watch him fly,

electric, brilliant blue—
beneath, he is orange, like flame—
colours I can't believe are so:

as legendary flowers bloom
incendiary in tint, a focal point
like Adams in a room.

Adams is like a bird;
alert (high on his pinnacle of air
he does not hear you, someone said);

in appearance he is bird-eyed
the bones of his face are
like the hollow bones of a bird.

And he stood by the elegant wall
between two pictures hanging there
certain of homage from us all;

as through the mind this minute
he draws the universe
and like our admiration, dresses in it,

towering like the cliffs of this coast
with his stiletto wing
and orange on his breast;

sucked up, utterly drained
the colours of my sea,
the yellow of this tidal ground;

swallowing all my thought,
swallows all those dark fish there
whom a rock hides from sunlight . . .

Till Rest, cries my mind to Adams' ghost,
only go elsewhere, let me alone
creep into the dead bird, cease to exist.

Nathanya, Palestine, 1942

THE OFFENSIVE

I

Tonight's a moonlit cup
and holds the liquid time
that will run out in flame
in poison we shall sup.

The moon's at home in a passion
of foreboding. Her lord
the martial sun, abroad
this month will see Time fashion

the action we begin
and Time will cage again
the devils we let run
whether we lose or win:

in the month's dregs will
a month hence some descry
the too late prophecy
of what the month lets fall.

This overture of quiet
is a minute to think on
the quiet like a curtain
when the piece is complete.

So in conjecture stands
my starlit body; the mind
mobile as a fox sneaks round
the sleepers waiting for their wounds.

This overture of quiet
is a minute to think on
the quiet like a curtain
when the piece is complete.

II

The stars dead heroes in the sky
may well approve the way you die
nor will the sun
revile those who survive because
for the dying and promising there was
these evils remain:

when you are dead and the harm done
the orators and clerks go on
the rulers of interims and wars
effete and stable as stars.

The stars in their fragile house
are the heavenly symbols of a class
dead in their seats,
and the officious sun goes round
organizing life; and what he's planned
Time comes and eats.

The sun goes round and the stars go round
the nature of eternity is circular
and man must spend his life to find
all our successes and failures are similar.

Wadi Natrun, 1942

I LISTEN TO THE DESERT WIND

I listen to the desert wind
that will not blow her from my mind;
the stars will not put down a hand,
the moon's ignorant of my wound

moving negligently across
by clouds and cruel tracts of space
as in my brain by nights and days
moves the reflection of her face.

Skims like a bird my sleepless eye
the sands who at this hour deny
the violent heat they have by day
as she denies her former way:

all the elements agree
with her, to have no sympathy
for my tactless misery
as wonderful and hard as she.

O turn in the dark bed again
and give to him what once was mine
and I'll turn as you turn
and kiss my swarthy mistress pain.

Wadi Natrun, 1942

THE KNIFE

Can I explain this to you? Your eyes
are entrances the mouths of caves—
I issue from wonderful interiors
upon a blessed sea and a fine day,
from inside these caves I look and dream.

Your hair explicable as a waterfall
in some black liquid cooled by legend
fell across my thought in a moment,
became a garment I am naked without,
lines drawn across through morning and evening.

And in your body each minute I died;
moving your thigh could disinter me
from a grave in a distant city:
your breasts deserted by cloth, clothed in twilight
filled me with tears, sweet cups of flesh.

Yes, to touch two fingers made us worlds,
stars, waters, promontories, chaos,
swooning in elements without form or time
come down through long seas among sea marvels
embracing like survivors on our islands.

This I think happened to us together
though now no shadow of it flickers in your hands,
your eyes look down on banal streets.
If I talk to you I might be a bird
with a message, a dead man, a photograph.

October 18th, 1942

SONG

Do I venture away too far
from the hot coast of your love
whose southern virtues charmed me?
How long how long can I be safe,
for the poisonous sea and a cruel star
the one by day and one at night have charmed me.

And are you troubled with a fear
that I must be a seastruck lad
or that the devil armed me
with a compass in my head?
for the poisonous sea and a cruel star
the one by day and one at night have charmed me.

At night I see the hissing fire
when star and sea communicate
and they have alarmed me
by their interest and hate
for the poisonous sea and a cruel star
the one by day and one at night have charmed me.

O listen to the ship and hear
she sings all night a sailors' rune;
since the green water's claimed me
harm is coming to her soon
for the poisonous sea and a cruel star
the one by day and one at night have charmed me.

Yes, for I am doomed my dear
and I have jilted myself and you;
soon when the sea's embalmed me
I'll fade into the deceitful blue,
for the poisonous sea and a cruel star
the one by day and one at night have charmed me.

1942

DEVILS

My mind's silence is not that of a wood
warm and full of the sun's patience,
who peers through the leaves waiting
perhaps the arrival of a god,
silence I welcomed when I could:
but this deceptive quiet is
the fastening of a soundproof trap
whose idiot crew must not escape.
Only within they make their noise;
all night, against my sleep, their cries.
Outside the usual crowd of devils
are flying in the clouds, are running
on the earth, imperceptibly spinning
through the black air alive with evils
and turning, diving in the wind's channels.
Inside the unsubstantial wall
these idiots of the mind can't hear
the demons talking in the air
who think my mind void. That's all;
there'll be an alliance of devils if it fall.

Egypt, 1942

EGYPT

Aniseed has a sinful taste:
at your elbow a woman's voice
like, I imagine, the voice of ghosts,
demanding food. She has no grace

but, diseased and blind of an eye
and heavy with habitual dolour,
listlessly finds you and I
and the table are the same colour.

The music, the harsh talk, the fine
clash of the drinkseller's tray,
are the same to her, as her own whine;
she knows no variety.

And in fifteen years of living
found nothing different from death
but the difference of moving
and the nuisance of breath.

A disguise of ordure can't hide
her beauty, succumbing in a cloud
of disease, disease, apathy. My God,
the king of this country must be proud.

Egypt, 1942

CHRISTODOULOS

Christodoulos moves, and shakes
his seven chins. He is that freak
a successful alchemist, and makes
God knows how much a week.

Out of Christodoulos' attic,
full of smoke and smells, emerge
soldiers like ants; with ants' erratic
gestures seek the pavement's verge;

weak as wounded, leaning in a knot,
shout in the streets for an enemy—
the dross of Christodoulos' pot
or wastage from his alchemy.

They flow elsewhere; by swarthy portals
entering the crucibles of others
and the lesser sages' mortars:
but Christodoulos is the father

of all; he's the original wise one
from whose experiments they told
how War can be the famous stone
for turning rubbish into gold.

Egypt, 1942

Sweat lines the statue of a face
he has; he looks at the sea
and does not smell its animal smell
does not suspect the heaven or hell
in the mind of a passer-by:
sees the moon shining on a place

in the sea, leans on the railing, rests
a hot hand on the eared rifle-muzzle,
nodding to the monotone of his song
his tarbrush with its khaki cover on.
There is no pain, no pleasure, life's no puzzle
but a standing, a leaning, a sleep between the coasts

of birth and dying. From mother's shoulder
to crawling in the rich gutter, millionaire of smells,
standing, leaning at last with seizing limbs
into the gutter again, while the world swims
on stinks and noises past the filthy wall
and death lifts him to the bearer's shoulder.

The moon shines on the modern flats
where sentient lovers or rich couples
lie loving or sleeping after eating.
In the town the cafés and cabarets seating
gossipers, soldiers, drunkards, supple
women of the town, shut out the moon with slats.

Everywhere is a real or artificial race
of life, a struggle of everyone to be
master or mistress of some hour.
But of this no scent or sound reaches him there.
He leans and looks at the sea:
sweat lines the statue of a face.

L'AUTOBUS

The motorbus in the Rue Malika Nazli
motorbus of the school of the Incarnation
making bulldog grunts in its nose
turns out into the Saturday traffic whose
diverging streams embrace the white policeman.
The twenty-six young girls stare busily

conjecturing, twittering, out of eyes
black, grey, brown, violet, nocturnal blue
of a dozen countries. Their mothers' mothers were
perhaps Odysseus' bondwomen, the fair
women of the Troad, Tunisians, Syrians who
for centuries mingled with the swarthy coastwise

seamen, variegated women of the ports
and seabounded villages of many tongues
among the gulls' cries. Probably eyed ships
carried these children's ancestors on trade trips
among the wine-dark sea's white towns
famous for beauty and nefarious arts.

Now under the nun's eye they sit,
the neutralizing beam of holiness;
their touring eyes, ignorant of love or pain
to come, watch eagerly the intriguing game,
street counterplay of virtue and wickedness
in which their mothers were so versed, so adept.

BEHAVIOUR OF FISH IN AN EGYPTIAN
TEA GARDEN

As a white stone draws down the fish
she on the seafloor of the afternoon
draws down men's glances and their cruel wish
for love. Slyly red lip on the spoon

slips in a morsel of ice-cream; her hands
white as a milky stone, white submarine
fronds, sink with spread fingers, lean
along the table, carmined at the ends.

A cotton magnate, an important fish
with great eyepouches and a golden mouth
through the frail reefs of furniture swims out
and idling, suspended, stays to watch.

A crustacean old man clamped to his chair
sits coldly near her and might see
her charms through fissures where the eyes should be
or else his teeth are parted in a stare.

Captain on leave, a lean dark mackerel,
lies in the offing; turns himself and looks
through currents of sound. The flat-eyed flatfish sucks
on a straw, staring from its repose, laxly.

And gallants in shoals swim up and lag,
circling and passing near the white attraction:
sometimes pausing, opening a conversation;
fish pause so to nibble or tug.

Now the ice-cream is finished, is
paid for. The fish swim off on business
and she sits alone at the table, a white stone
useless except to a collector, a rich man.

Cairo, 8th October, 1943

SNAKESKIN AND STONE

I praise a snakeskin or a stone:
a bald head or a public speech
I hate: the serpent's lozenges
are a calligraphy, and it is
truth these cryptograms teach,
the pebble is truth alone.
Complication belonging to the snake
who is as subtle as his gold, black, green—
it is right the stone is old
and smooth, utterly cruel and old.
These two are two pillars. Between
stand all the buildings truth can make,
a whole city, inhabited by lovers,
murderers, workmen and artists
not much recognized: all
who have no memorial
but are mere men. Even the lowest
never made himself a mask of words or figures.
The bald head is a desert
between country of life and country of death;
between the desolate projecting ears
move the wicked explorers, the flies
who know the dead bone is beneath
and from the skin the life half out
and dead words tumbled in heaps
in the papers lie in rows
awaiting burial. The speakers mouth
like a cold sea that sucks and spews them out
with insult to their bodies. Tangled they cruise
like mariners' bodies in the grave of ships.
Borrow hair for the bald crown,
borrow applause for the dead words;
for you who think the desert hidden
or the words, like the dry bones, living
are fit to profit from the world.
And God help the lover of snakeskin and stone.

CAIRO JAG

Shall I get drunk or cut myself a piece of cake,
a pasty Syrian with a few words of English
or the Turk who says she is a princess—she dances
apparently by levitation? Or Marcelle, Parisienne
always preoccupied with her dull dead lover:
she has all the photographs and his letters
tied in a bundle and stamped *Décédé* in mauve ink.
All this takes place in a stink of jasmin.

But there are the streets dedicated to sleep
stenches and sour smells, the sour cries
do not disturb their application to slumber
all day, scattered on the pavement like rags
afflicted with fatalism and hashish. The women
offering their children brown-paper breasts
dry and twisted, elongated like the skull,
Holbein's signature. But this stained white town
is something in accordance with mundane conventions—
Marcelle drops her Gallic airs and tragedy
suddenly shrieks in Arabic about the fare
with the cabman, links herself so
with the somnambulists and legless beggars:
it is all one, all as you have heard.

But by a day's travelling you reach a new world
the vegetation is of iron
dead tanks, gun barrels split like celery
the metal brambles have no flowers or berries
and there are all sorts of manure, you can imagine
the dead themselves, their boots, and possessions
clinging to the ground, a man with no head
has a packet of chocolate and a souvenir of Tripoli.

DEAD MEN

Tonight the moon inveigles them
to love: they infer from her gaze
her tacit encouragement.
Tonight the white dresses and the jasmin scent
in the streets. I in another place
see the white dresses glimmer like moths. Come

to the west, out of that trance, my heart—
here the same hours have illumined
sleepers who are condemned or reprieved
and those whom their ambitions have deceived;
the dead men whom the wind
powders till they are like dolls: they tonight

rest in the sanitary earth perhaps
or where they died, no one has found them
or in their shallow graves the wild dog
discovered and exhumed a face or a leg
for food: the human virtue round them
is a vapour tasteless to a dog's chops.

All that is good of them, the dog consumes.
You would not know now the mind's flame is gone
more than the dog knows: you would forget
but that you see your own mind burning yet
and till you stifle in the ground will go on
burning the economical coal of your dreams.

Then leave the dead in the earth, an organism
not capable of resurrection, like mines,
less durable than the metal of a gun,
a casual meal for a dog, nothing but the bone
so soon. But tonight no lovers see the lines
of the moon's face as the lines of cynicism.

And the wise man is the lover
who in his planetary love resolves
without the traction of reason or time's control
and the wild dog finding meat in a hole
is a philosopher. The prudent mind resolves
on the lover's or the dog's attitude forever.

MERSA

This blue half circle of sea
moving transparently
on sand as pale as salt
was Cleopatra's hotel:

here is a guest house built
and broken utterly since.
An amorous modern prince
lived in this scoured shell.

Now from the skeletal town
the cherry-skinned soldiers stroll down
to undress to idle on the white beach.
Up there, the immensely long road goes by

to Tripoli: the wind and dust reach
the secrets of the whole
poor town whose masks would still
deceive a passer-by;

faces with sightless doors
for eyes, with cracks like tears
oozing at corners. A dead tank alone
leans where the gossips stood.

I see my feet like stones
underwater. The logical little fish
converge and nip the flesh
imagining I am one of the dead.

WORDS

Words are my instruments but not my servants;
by the white pillar of a prince I lie in wait
for them. In what the hour or the minute invents,
in a web formally meshed or inchoate,
these fritillaries are come upon, trapped:
hot-coloured, or the cold scarabs a thousand years
old, found in cerements and unwrapped.
The catch and the ways of catching are diverse.
For instance this stooping man, the bones of whose face are
like the hollow birds' bones, is a trap for words.
And the pockmarked house bleached by the glare
whose insides war has dried out like gourds
attracts words. There are those who capture them
in hundreds, keep them prisoners in black
bottles, release them at exercise and clap them back.
But I keep words only a breath of time
turning in the lightest of cages—uncover
and let them go: sometimes they escape for ever.

El Ballah, 1943

119

GALLANTRY

The colonel in a casual voice
spoke into the microphone a joke
which through a hundred earphones broke
into the ears of a doomed race.

Into the ears of the doomed boy, the fool
whose perfectly mannered flesh fell
in opening the door for a shell
as he had learnt to do at school.

Conrad luckily survived the winter:
he wrote a letter to welcome
the suspicious spring: only his silken
intentions severed with a single splinter.

Was George fond of little boys?
we always suspected it,
but who will say: since George was hit
we never mention our surmise.

It was a brave thing the colonel said,
but the whole sky turned too hot
and the three heroes never heard what
it was, gone deaf with steel and lead.

But the bullets cried with laughter,
the shells were overcome with mirth,
plunging their heads in steel and earth—
(the air commented in a whisper).

El Ballah, General Hospital, 1943

VERGISSMEINICHT

Three weeks gone and the combatants gone,
returning over the nightmare ground
we found the place again, and found
the soldier sprawling in the sun.

The frowning barrel of his gun
overshadowing. As we came on
that day, he hit my tank with one
like the entry of a demon.

Look. Here in the gunpit spoil
the dishonoured picture of his girl
who has put: *Steffi. Vergissmeinicht*
in a copybook gothic script.

We see him almost with content
abased, and seeming to have paid
and mocked at by his own equipment
that's hard and good when he's decayed.

But she would weep to see today
how on his skin the swart flies move;
the dust upon the paper eye
and the burst stomach like a cave.

For here the lover and killer are mingled
who had one body and one heart.
And death who had the soldier singled
has done the lover mortal hurt.

Homs, Tripolitania, 1943

HOW TO KILL

Under the parabola of a ball,
a child turning into a man,
I looked into the air too long.
The ball fell in my hand, it sang
in the closed fist: *Open Open*
Behold a gift designed to kill.

Now in my dial of glass appears
the soldier who is going to die.
He smiles, and moves about in ways
his mother knows, habits of his.
The wires touch his face: I cry
NOW. Death, like a familiar, hears

and look, has made a man of dust
of a man of flesh. This sorcery
I do. Being damned, I am amused
to see the centre of love diffused
and the waves of love travel into vacancy.
How easy it is to make a ghost.

The weightless mosquito touches
her tiny shadow on the stone,
and with how like, how infinite
a lightness, man and shadow meet.
They fuse. A shadow is a man
when the mosquito death approaches.

Tunisia-Cairo, 1943

ENFIDAVILLE

In the church fallen like dancers
lie the Virgin and St. Thérèse
on little pillows of dust.
The detonations of the last few days
tore down the ornamental plasters
shivered the hands of Christ.

The men and women who moved like candles
in and out of the houses and the streets
are all gone. The white houses are bare
black cages. No one is left to greet
the ghosts tugging at doorhandles
opening doors that are not there.

Now the daylight coming in from the fields
like a labourer, tired and sad,
is peering about among the wreckage, goes
past some corners as though with averted head
not looking at the pain this town holds,
seeing no one move behind the windows.

But already they are coming back; to search
like ants, poking in the débris, finding in it
a bed or a piano and carrying it out.
Who would not love them at this minute?
I seem again to meet
The blue eyes of the images in the church.

Tunisia, 1943

ARISTOCRATS

'I think I am becoming a God'

The noble horse with courage in his eye
clean in the bone, looks up at a shellburst:
away fly the images of the shires
but he puts the pipe back in his mouth.

Peter was unfortunately killed by an 88:
it took his leg away, he died in the ambulance.
I saw him crawling on the sand; he said
It's most unfair, they've shot my foot off.

How can I live among this gentle
obsolescent breed of heroes, and not weep?
Unicorns, almost,
for they are falling into two legends
in which their stupidity and chivalry
are celebrated. Each, fool and hero, will be an
    immortal.

The plains were their cricket pitch
and in the mountains the tremendous drop fences
brought down some of the runners. Here then
under the stones and earth they dispose themselves,
I think with their famous unconcern.
It is not gunfire I hear but a hunting horn.

Enfidaville, Tunisia, 1943

I EXPERIMENT

The shadows of leaves falling like minutes
seascapes discoveries of sea creatures
and voices out of the extreme distance reach us
like conjured sounds Faces cruising like spirits

across the backward glance of the brain
In the bowl of the mind a pot pourri
Such shapes and colours become a lurid
décor to the adventures that are a cycle When

I play dancers choreographers critics rôle
I see myself dance happiness and pain
(each as illusory as rain)
in silence Silence Break it with the small

isolated tinkle the apathetic buzz buzz
pirouetting into a crescendo BANG until
as each scene closes hush the stage is still
Everything is where it was

The finale if it should come is
the moment my love and I meet
our hands move out across a room of strangers
certain they hold the rose of love

Egypt, October, 1943

THE TRUMPET

O how after Arcturus
have you and your companions
heard the laughter and the distant shout
of this long tube a man sets to his mouth
crying that war is sweet, and the men you
see asleep after fighting will fight in the day before us?

Since with manual skill
men dressed to kill in purple
with how many strange tongues
cried the trumpet, that cried once
for the death of Hector from Troy steeple
that cried when a hundred hopes fell.

Tonight we heard it
who for weeks have only listened
to the howls of inhuman voices.
But, as the apprehensive ear rejoiced
breathing the notes in, the sky glistened
with a flight of bullets. We must be up early

tomorrow, to forget the cry and the crier
as we forgot the conversation
of our friends killed last month, last week
and hear, crouching, the air shriek
the crescendo, expectancy to elation
violently arriving. The trumpet is a liar.

Middle East R.A.C. Base Depot

LANDSCAPE WITH FIGURES

I

Perched on a great fall of air
a pilot or angel looking down
on some eccentric chart, the plain
dotted with the useless furniture
discerns crouching on the sand vehicles
squashed dead or still entire, stunned
like beetles: scattered wingcases and
legs, heads, show when the haze settles.
But you who like Thomas come
to poke fingers in the wounds
find monuments, and metal posies:
on each disordered tomb
the steel is torn into fronds
by the lunatic explosive.

II

On scrub and sand the dead men wriggle
in their dowdy clothes. They are mimes
who express silence and futile aims
enacting this prone and motionless struggle
at a queer angle to the scenery
crawling on the boards of the stage like walls,
deaf to the one who opens his mouth and calls
silently. The décor is terrible tracery
of iron. The eye and mouth of each figure
bear the cosmetic blood and hectic
colours death has the only list of.
A yard more, and my little finger
could trace the maquillage of these stony actors;
I am the figure writhing on the backcloth.

III

I am the figure burning in hell
and the figure of the grave priest
observing everyone who passed
and that of the lover. I am all
the aimless pilgrims, the pedants and courtiers:
more easily you believe me a pioneer
and a murdering villain without fear
without remorse hacking at the throat. Yes,
I am all these and I am the craven
the remorseful the distressed
penitent: not passing from life to life
but all these angels and devils are driven
into my mind like beasts. I am possessed,
the house whose wall contains the dark strife
the arguments of hell with heaven.

Middle East R.A.C. Base Depot

On a return from Egypt

To stand here in the wings of Europe
disheartened, I have come away
from the sick land where in the sun lay
the gentle sloe-eyed murderers
of themselves, exquisites under a curse;
here to exercise my depleted fury.

For the heart is a coal, growing colder
when jewelled cerulean seas change
into grey rocks, grey water-fringe,
sea and sky altering like a cloth
till colours and sheen are gone both:
cold is an opiate of the soldier.

And all my endeavours are unlucky explorers
come back, abandoning the expedition;
the specimens, the lilies of ambition
still spring in their climate still unpicked:
but time, time is all I lacked
to find them, as the great collectors before me.

The next month, then, is a window
and with a crash I'll split the glass.
Behind it stands one I must kiss,
person of love or death
a person or a wraith,
I fear what I shall find.

Keith Douglas.

Holograph of the last poem completed
by Keith Douglas

DESERT FLOWERS

Living in a wide landscape are the flowers—
Rosenberg I only repeat what you were saying—
the shell and the hawk every hour
are slaying men and jerboas, slaying

the mind: but the body can fill
the hungry flowers and the dogs who cry words
at nights, the most hostile things of all.
But that is not new. Each time the night discards

draperies on the eyes and leaves the mind awake
I look each side of the door of sleep
for the little coin it will take
to buy the secret I shall not keep.

I see men as trees suffering
or confound the detail and the horizon.
Lay the coin on my tongue and I will sing
of what the others never set eyes on.

Egypt, 1943

ON A RETURN FROM EGYPT

To stand here in the wings of Europe
disheartened, I have come away
from the sick land where in the sun lay
the gentle sloe-eyed murderers
of themselves, exquisites under a curse;
here to exercise my depleted fury.

For the heart is a coal, growing colder
when jewelled cerulean seas change
into grey rocks, grey water-fringe,
sea and sky altering like a cloth
till colours and sheen are gone both:
cold is an opiate of the soldier.

And all my endeavours are unlucky explorers
come back, abandoning the expedition;
the specimens, the lilies of ambition
still spring in their climate, still unpicked:
but time, time is all I lacked
to find them, as the great collectors before me.

The next month, then, is a window
and with a crash I'll split the glass.
Behind it stands one I must kiss,
person of love or death
a person or a wraith,
I fear what I shall find.

Egypt-England, 1943–44

TRANSLATIONS

What lissom boy among the roses,
Sprinkled with liquid scents, proposes
To court you in your grotto, fair
Pyrrha? For whom is your blond hair

Bound with plain art? Alas, how often
Will he bid changèd gods to soften;
Till, poor landlubber, he finds
The sea is rough with inky winds,

Who now, poor gull, enjoys you gold,
And always carefree, always bold
To love, hopes on and never knows
The gold is tinsel: wretched those

For whom you shine untried. For me,
Grateful to the great god of the sea,
A votive tablet will recall
Drenched garments on his temple wall.

1940

HEAD OF A FAUN

(From the French of Arthur Rimbaud)

In the foliage, a green casket spotty with gold,
In the green foliage indefinite, and all flowery
With splendid flowers where a kiss is curled
Alive, and bursts their exquisite embroidery,

A wild faun shows his two eyes
And bites, in his white teeth, the red flowers:
Tanned and full-blooded as an ancient wine,
Under the branches his lip curls in laughters.

And when like a squirrel he has run away free,
His laughter yet trembles on every leaf;
Made finer by a bullfinch you may see
The bosky golden kiss in new relief.

1940

AU CABARET-VERT

(From the French of Arthur Rimbaud)

For eight days I had worn my boots out
on the cobbles of streets. I entered Charleroi
and at the Cabaret-Vert bespoke a cut
of bread and butter, some warm ham, no more.

Content, I stretched my legs under the green table
and contemplated the ingenuous designs
of the carpet. Also it was delectable
when the girl with the enormous breasts and sparkling eyes—

—she wouldn't be frightened of a kiss, that girl—
brought me my bread and butter all with a smile,
some warm ham in a decorated plate,

some pink and white ham, touched with a perfume
of garlic; and filled me a great glass, its foam
gilt with a glimmer of belated sunlight.

1940

LE DORMEUR DU VAL

(From the French of Arthur Rimbaud, 1870)

It is a hollow of verdure with a brook singing
which distractedly with rags of silver arrays
the grass; where the sun in pride across the mountain
sparkles. It is a vale effervescent with rays.

A young soldier with bare head and mouth open
and his neck immersed in the fresh blue flowers
is sleeping stretched out in grass under heaven
pale in his green bed where the light showers.

His feet in swordgrass, he sleeps smiling. So
smiles a sick child. He is fallen in a doze.
Nature, attend and warm him, he is cold.

These scents will not succeed to charm
his nostrils. Asleep in sunlight with his arm
across him. On the right side are two red holes.

UNFINISHED POEMS AND FRAGMENTS

TO
KRISTIN
YINGCHENG
OLGA
MILENA

Women of four countries
the four phials full of essences
of green England, legendary China,
cold Europe, Arabic Spain, a finer
four poisons for the subtle senses
than any in mediaeval inventories.

Here I give back perforce
the sweet wine to the grape
give the dark plant its juices
what every creature uses
by natural law will seep
back to the natural source.

TEL AVIV

Like Ophelia in a pool of shadow lies
your face, flower that draws down my lips;
our hands meet like strangers in a city
among the glasses on the table tops
impervious to envy or pity—
we two lost in the country of our eyes.

In your locked mind your news from Russia is
and if I think there is waiting Libya
Tripoli; the many heads of war
are watching us. We are not unaware,
but are this evening finding heavier
than war the scents of youth, youth's subtleties.

We who cannot put out a single hand
to help our balance, who can never lean
on an old building in the past
or a new building in the future, must
balance tiptoe on a pin,
could teach an angel how to stand.

Do not laugh because I have made a poem;
it is to use what then we could not handle
words too dangerous then, knowing their explosive
or incendiary tendencies when we are so close—
if I had said this to you then, BANG will
have gone our walls of indifference in flame.

The noise of people surrounds us
the sky encloses the whole city
bending over like a dark theatre
islanded, we smile and wonder
how permanent and rare the petty
talk and laughter of the dancers.

SATURDAY EVENING IN JERUSALEM

In summer evenings the moonstruck city fills
with movement of people, tides of speech
and the whole evening moving where
the words stream down into the square;
the street is full of shoulders. Watch
moonlight leap out between the hotels.

Young men and girls linked in fours and twos
under the moon sitting so high so bright
are drawn uphill between the figures of trees
now softening hot walls appear to freeze
and silver children go in and out
stumping on the pavements with their shoes.

It is a collaboration between things
and people; the cat moonlight prowling about
rubs against friendly legs, leaps upon
the shoulders of a family. Family song,
incense of talk and laughter mounting the night;
in the dome of stars the moon sings.

But among these Jews I am the Jew
the outcast, wandering down the steep road
into the hostile dark square:
and standing in the unlit corner here
know I am alone and cursed by God
as if lost on my first morning at school.

I WATCH WITH INTEREST,
FOR THEY ARE GHOSTS

I

I watch with interest, for they are ghosts
shaken by their fealty to the past
into a mood of sorrow and veneration
and with the hand of pity at my eyes
their gestures, those in their rich lifetime were
the mark of their nobility and merit.
Support and picture in their proper gear
these skeletons of conversation falling
from the lips of a nobleman or king
while still we recall what nobles and kings were.

II

As I watch each closely—for they are ghosts
and grow invisible before our eyes
I feel the hand of pity on my heart
shaken by their fealty to the past. Look,
their gestures. These in their rich lifetime bore
the mark of their nobility and pride.
Can you apparel in their proper gear
these skeletons of conversation falling
from the lips of a dead nobleman or king
while still we know what nobles and kings were.

London, 1944

Actors waiting in the wings of Europe
we already watch the lights on the stage
and listen to the colossal overture begin.
For us entering at the height of the din
it will be hard to hear our thoughts, hard to gauge
how much our conduct owes to fear or fury.

Everyone, I suppose, will use these minutes
to look back, to hear music and recall
what we were doing and saying that year
during our last few months as people, near
the sucking mouth of the day that swallowed us all
into the stomach of a war. Now we are in it

and no more people, just little pieces of food
swirling in an uncomfortable digestive journey.
What we said and did then has a slightly
fairytale quality. There is an excitement
in seeing our ghosts wandering.

BÊTE NOIRE

The trumpet swings out to blow you off the isle and dancers

I

The trumpet man to take it away
blows a hot break in a beautiful way
ought to snap my fingers and tap my toes
but I sit at my table and nobody knows
I've got a beast on my back.

A mediaeval animal with a dog's face
Notre Dame or Chartres is his proper place
but here he is in the Piccadilly
sneering at the hot musicians' skill. He
is the beast on my back.

Suppose we dance, suppose we run away
into the street, or the underground
he'd come with us. It's his day.
Don't kiss me. Don't put your arm round
and touch the beast on my back.

II

This is my particular monster, I know him;
he walks about inside me: I'm his house
and his landlord. He's my evacuee
taking a respite from hell in me
he decorates his room of course
to remind him of home. He often talks of going

Such a persuasive gentleman he is
I believe him, I go out quite sure
that I'll come back and find him gone
but does he go? Not him. No, he's a one
who likes his joke, he won't sit waiting for
me to come home, but comes

III

Yes, I too have a particular monster
a toad or a worm curled in the belly
stirring, eating at times I cannot foretell, he
is the thing I can admit only once to
anyone, never to those who have not their own.

Never to those who are happy, whose easy language
I speak well, though with a stranger's accent.

IV

If at times my eyes are lenses
through which the brain explores
constellations of feeling
my ears yielding like swinging doors
admit princes to the corridors
into the mind, do not envy me.
I have a beast on my back.

London, 1944

NOTES

NOTES

Two statements by Keith Douglas on Poetry are in existence and it has been thought of interest to include them here.

The first, entitled 'On the Nature of Poetry', was written by the author for inclusion in a small symposium on that subject contained in the anthology *Augury: An Oxford Miscellany of Verse and Prose* edited by Alec M. Hardie and Keith C. Douglas (Basil Blackwell, 1940).

ON THE NATURE OF POETRY

'Poetry is like a man, whom thinking you know all his movements and appearance you will presently come upon in such a posture that for a moment you can hardly believe it a position of the limbs you know. So thinking you have set bounds to the nature of poetry, you shall as soon discover something outside your bounds which they should evidently contain.

'The expression "bad poetry" is meaningless: critics still use it, forgetting that bad poetry is not poetry at all.

'Nor can prose and poetry be compared any more than pictures and pencils: the one is instrument and the other art. Poetry may be written in prose or verse, or spoken extempore.

'For it is anything expressed in words, which appeals to the emotions either in presenting an image or picture to move them; or by the music of words affecting them through the senses; or in stating some truth whose eternal quality exacts the same reverence as eternity itself.

'In its nature poetry is sincere and simple.

'Writing which is poetry must say what the writer has himself to say, not what he has observed others to say with effect, nor what he thinks will impress his hearers because it impressed him hearing it. Nor must he waste any more words over it than a mathematician: every word must work for its keep, in prose, blank verse, or rhyme.

'And poetry is to be judged not by what the poet has tried to say; only by what he has said.'

The second statement is contained in a letter written by Keith Douglas to J. C. Hall. It is dated 10th August, 1943.

'. . . Incidentally you say I fail as a poet, when you mean I fail as a lyricist. Only someone who is out of touch, by which I mean first hand touch, with what has happened outside England—and from a cultural point of view I wish it had affected English life more— could make that criticism. I am surprised you should still expect me to produce musical verse. A lyric form and a lyric approach will do even less good than a journalese approach to the subjects we have to discuss now. I don't know if you have come across the word Bullshit— it is an army word and signifies humbug and unnecessary detail. It symbolizes what I think must be got rid of—the mass of irrelevancies, of "attitudes," "approaches", propaganda, ivory towers, etc., that stands between us and our problems and what we have to do about them. To write on the themes which have been concerning me lately in lyric and abstract form would be immense bullshitting.

'In my early poems I wrote lyrically, as an innocent, because I was an innocent: I have (not surprisingly) fallen from that particular grace since then. I had begun to change during my second year at Oxford. T. S. Eliot wrote to me when I first joined the Army, that I appeared to have finished with one form of writing and to be progressing to- wards another, which he did not think I had mastered. I knew this to be true without his saying it. Well, I am still changing: I don't disagree with you if you say I am awkward and not used to the new paces yet. But my object (and I don't give a damn about my duty as a poet) is to write true things, significant things in words each of which works for its place in a line. My rhythms, which you find enervated, are carefully chosen to enable the poems to be *read* as significant speech: I see no reason to be either musical or sonorous about things at present. When I do, I shall be so again, and glad to. I suppose I reflect the cynicism and the careful absence of expectation (it is not quite the same as apathy) with which I view the world. As many others to whom I have spoken, not only civilians and British soldiers, but Germans and Italians, are in the same state of mind, it is a true reflection. I never tried to write about war (that is battles and things, not London can Take it), with the exception of a satiric picture of some soldiers frozen to death, until I had experienced it. Now I will write of it, and perhaps one day cynic and lyric will meet and make me a balanced style. Certainly you will never see the long metrical similes and galleries of images again.

'Your talk of regrouping sounds to me—if you will excuse me for exhibiting a one-track mind—like the military excuse of a defeated general. There is never much need to regroup. Let your impulses drive you forward; never lose contact with life or you will lose the impulses as well. Meanwhile if you must regroup, do it by re-reading your old stuff.

'Of course, you will never take my advice nor I yours. But in these tirades a few ideas do scrape through the defences on either side. Perhaps all this may make it easier for you to understand why I am writing the way I am and why I shall never go back to the old forms. You may even begin to see some virtue in it. To be sentimental or emotional now is dangerous to oneself and to others. To trust anyone or to admit any hope of a better world is criminally foolish, as foolish as it is to stop working for it. It sounds silly to say work without hope, but it can be done; it's only a form of insurance; it doesn't mean work hopelessly.'

The remaining notes are not intended to provide a comprehensive list of alternative versions, nor a commentary; this would be tedious. On the other hand, where a text differs markedly from its appearance in some previous publication a note has been thought necessary. Similarly, where a genuine alternative or earlier version has an intrinsic interest of its own or where a poem contains some other matter of interest, a note has been added. In view of references to Douglas's war journal, *Alamein to Zem Zem,* it should perhaps be explained that the 1946 edition of that book contained the Middle East poems as a supplement.

BEXHILL (p. 32) was Keith Douglas's home where he lived with his mother from the age of twelve.

DEJECTION (p. 34). The version in *New Verse* has 'autumn's country' in the first line, but when later published by Douglas in *Cherwell* 'autumn' becomes 'summer', presumably to secure the contrast with 'autumn clothes'. The penultimate line is missing in the *Cherwell* version.

SONNET (p. 35). An earlier published version has 'draped rain' in the first line and 'Pattern'd and tinted picture' in the third.

VILLANELLE OF GORIZIA (p. 37). An alternative to lines 16 and 17 (the last verse) reads:

> 'O distant heat and music: if I might
> go back; after return my heart grieves.'

FORGOTTEN THE RED LEAVES (p. 43). Originally published under the title of 'Poem from a Sequence'. There is also a version called 'Pleasures'.

VILLANELLE OF SPRING BELLS (p. 58). In the 1951 collected edition the tenth and eleventh lines are incorrectly given as:

> 'Birds feel the enchantment of his wing
> and in ten fine notes dispel twenty cares.'

EXTENSION TO FRANCIS THOMPSON (p. 65). The *Cherwell* version from which this poem is taken reads for the last line:

> 'analysis in worshipping'.

On the authority of John Heath-Stubbs, however, who was present at the time, this alteration of 'is' to 'in' was made by Sidney Keyes, then Editor, without consulting the author.

RUSSIANS (p. 68). A MS of this poem ends with the following note: 'During the Russian campaign against Finland, a Russian regiment was reported to have been discovered frozen to death, the soldiers still holding their rifles ready to fire'.

A MIME (p. 69). Some versions in the penultimate line have 'catch' instead of 'cadge'. The latter was presumably an afterthought to secure the rhyme.

THE PRISONER (p. 81). Cheng was a girl (see the fragment: 'To Kristin Yingcheng Olga Milena'). In the 1951 collected edition line 9 has 'hundred years' and the last line reads:

> 'from the ambitious cruel bone'.

The present text is the correct one.

THE NEWS FROM EARTH (p. 82). In the 1951 collected edition the last line reads:

'so clearly science had made his own conclusion'.

That was what Douglas originally wrote. However, in the MS the line has been crossed out and the present version substituted. The previous editors had some doubt about the authenticity of this revision, but we are now satisfied it is in Douglas's hand.

THE HOUSE (p. 83). Another version appeared in *Poetry London,* but the present version is the correct one.

OXFORD (p. 85). Also entitled 'The City'. Written after Douglas had revisited Oxford on leave.

SYRIA I (p. 95). This was the version published by Douglas in Cairo. SYRIA II (p. 96) is probably the later revision.

THE SEA BIRD & ADAMS (p. 99–100). The latter is presumably the later version, though dates (often unreliable) on the MSS suggest otherwise. THE SEA BIRD was the version published by Douglas in Cairo.

THE OFFENSIVE (p. 102). Written in Egypt shortly before Montgomery's attack at Alamein and originally entitled 'Reflections of the New Moon in Sand'.

I LISTEN TO THE DESERT WIND (p. 104). A typescript version entitled 'Milena' also exists, but the textual differences are unimportant.

SNAKESKIN AND STONE (p. 114). This poem, obviously unrevised but probably complete, exists only in a pencilled MS on flimsy paper from which part of line 17 has been torn away.

'but are *mere* men. Even the lowest'.

The italicized word is a guess of the editors'.

CAIRO JAG (p. 115). This is the version in *Personal Landscape Anthology* and so presumably the one Douglas wished to preserve. In a MS version, however, the poem continues:

'There are new ethics here and fresh virtues.
We have our wise men and lawgivers
artists—for we discovered new arts:
I think some have new religions, and
there are socialites, the smart set, rulers
and little rulers. In all this dry land
the beautiful trees of metal
the noble dead whom we honour as companions
with every indignity, the music is loud or soft
as variable and unexpected as the swing bands
as the classical orchestra of Sculz in Cairo.

You do not gradually appreciate such qualities
but your mind will extend new hands. In a moment
will fall down like St. Paul in a blinding light
the soul suffers a miraculous change
you become a true inheritor of this altered planet.

I know, I see these men return
wandering like lost sounds [*sic*] in our dirty streets'

MERSA (p. 118). For line 9 the *Alamein to Zem Zem* (1946) version
substitutes the cliché:

'Now from the ruined hive of a town.'

but with no MS authority.

VERGISSMEINICHT (p. 121). This is the version published by Douglas
in his own lifetime in *Personal Landscape*: it was published also in the
Personal Landscape Anthology, the proofs of which he would have had
an opportunity of correcting—had he wished to do so—up till the time
of his death. It must therefore be taken as the authoritative text. The
Alamein to Zem Zem version (published in 1946) presents variants for
which there is slight authority apart from (in the third verse) a possible
early draft. The earlier MS is entitled 'The Lover' and there seems no
support for the title 'Elegy for an 88 Gunner' given the poem in
Alamein to Zem Zem. This *Alamein to Zem Zem* version prints verses 2,
3 and 4 as follows:

'The frowning barrel of his gun
overshadows him. As we came on
that day, he hit my tank with one
like the entry of a demon.

And smiling in the gunpit spoil
is a picture of his girl
who has written: *Steffi, Vergissmeinicht.*
in a copybook Gothic script.

We see him almost with content,
abased and seeming to have paid,
mocked by his durable equipment
that's hard and good when he's decayed.'

Douglas has a note on one manuscript:

> 'Mein Mund ist stumm, aber mein Aug'es spricht
> Und was es sagt ist kurz—Vergissmeinicht.
>
> STEFFI.'

('My mouth is dumb but my eye speaks and what it says is short—
Forget me not, Steffi.')

HOW TO KILL (p. 122). In some MSS this is called 'The Sniper'.

ARISTOCRATS (p. 124). There are three differing MS versions of this
poem. The one in *Alamein to Zem Zem* (1946) appears to have been
taken from all three but omits entirely the fine last line with its echo of
Roncesvalles. A version entitled 'Sportsmen' ends:

> 'Listen
> Against the bullet cries the simple horn.'

What appears to be the earliest rough version contains the additional
lines (after line 8):

> 'Peter, have you got a tourniquet on?
> No, I haven't, I suppose I ought to have really.'

There is a note in the poet's handwriting relating to this poem:
'Lt-Col. J. O. Player, killed in Tunisia, Enfidaville, February, 1943,
left £3,000 to the Beaufort Hunt, and directed that the incumbent of

the living in his gift should be a "man who approves of hunting, shooting, and all manly sports, which are the backbone of the nation".'

I EXPERIMENT (p. 125). The present version without punctuation has been chosen as definitive, but there is also a punctuated one on airgraph entitled 'This is the Dream'. This runs:

'The shadows of leaves falling like minutes.
Seascapes. Discoveries of sea creatures
and voices, out of the extreme distance, reach us
like conjured sounds. Faces that are spirits

cruise across the backward glance of the brain.
In the bowl of the mind is pot pourri.
Such shapes and hues become a lurid
décor to The Adventures. These are a cycle. When

I play dancer's choreographer's critic's rôle
I see myself dance happiness and pain
(each as illusory as rain)
in silence. Silence. Break it with the small

tinkle; apathetic buzz buzz
pirouetting into a crescendo, BANG. Until
as each scene closes hush the stage is still,
everything is where it was.

The finale if it should come is
the moment my love and I meet
our hands move out across a room of strangers
certain they hold the rose of love.'

THE TRUMPET (p. 126). This poem was sent by Douglas to *Personal Landscape*, but was not used at the time and only came to light again after the publication of the 1951 collected edition. It now appears in book form for the first time.

LANDSCAPE WITH FIGURES & DESERT FLOWERS (p. 127–29). In *Alamein to Zem Zem* (1946) these two poems are joined together under the title of the latter. There appears to be no authority for this. The poems invariably exist in different MSS, 'Desert Flowers' was always published separately by Douglas in Cairo, and the date on an airgraph shows there to have been a interval of several months between the two poems.

Since the publication of the 1951 collected edition a new version of LANDSCAPE WITH FIGURES has come to light (it had apparently, like 'The Trumpet', been sent to *Personal Landscape* but not been used). The fact that it contains an extra (third) section suggests that this was Douglas's definitive version, and so we have decided to use it here. The first two sections differ only very slightly from the earlier version.

ON A RETURN FROM EGYPT (p. 130). This is believed to be the last poem Douglas completed before his death (although he was probably working later on the fragmentary 'Bête Noire'). An earlier version is called 'Misgiving'.

LE DORMEUR DU VAL (p. 133). Later the author was reminded of this poem of Rimbaud when he saw a dead Libyan soldier in the desert. (See *Alamein to Zem Zem.*)

TO KRISTIN YINGCHENG OLGA MILENA (p. 139). In the 1951 collected edition the first name was given incorrectly as Kaistin. Another version of this fragment runs:

> 'Women of four countries
> the four phials full of essences
> of green England, legendary China,
> deep Europe and Arabic Spain, a
> finer four poisons for the five senses
> than any in mediaeval inventories.
>
> In giving you this I
> return the wine to the grape
> return the plant her juices
> for what each creature uses
> by chemistry will seep
> back to the source or die.'

TEL-A-VIV & SATURDAY EVENING IN JERUSALEM (p. 140–41). A fragment headed 'Jerusalem' suggests that Douglas, finding both these poems unsatisfactory, intended to join their parts together. It reads:

'Tonight there is a movement of things
the cat moonlight leaps out
between the dark hotels upon
the rivers of people; is gone
and in the dark words fall about.
In the dome of stars the moon sings

Ophelia, in a pool of shadow lies
your face, flower that draws down my lips
our hands meet like strangers in a city
among the glasses on the table-top
impervious to envy or pity
we two lost in the country of our eyes.

We two, and other twos.
Stalingrad, Pacific, Tunis,
Tripoli, the many heads of war
are watching us. But now, and here
is night's short forgiveness
that all lovers use.

Now the'

I WATCH WITH INTEREST, FOR THEY ARE GHOSTS. (p. 142). Two versions of the same fragment. A further rendering reads:

'Shaken by such a fealty to the past
to fix their picture (they are all ghosts
I watch these lunatics whose fancy is
that they are living. Heavens, what a grace
the attractive pitiful delusion has,
how like the living in their proper gear
their skeletons of conversation falling
from the dead lips of a gentleman or a king.

As at their final dance, I look jealously
to fix their picture (they are all ghosts
and turn invisible each moment.'

ACTORS WAITING IN THE WINGS OF EUROPE (p. 143). Another version of this fragment contains much of what later became the poem 'On a Return from Egypt'.

BÊTE NOIRE (p. 144). The poem that Douglas was never able to finish. In this connection he has left the following 'Note on Drawing for the Jacket of Bête Noire'.

'Bête Noire is the name of the poem I can't write; a protracted failure, which is also a protracted success I suppose. Because it is the poem I begin to write in a lot of other poems: this is what justifies my use of that title for the book.

'The beast, which I have drawn as black care sitting behind the horseman, is indefinable: sitting down to try and describe it, I have sensations of physical combat, and after five hours of writing last night, which resulted in failure, all my muscles were tired. But if he is not caught, at least I can see his tracks (anyone may see them), in some of the other poems. My failure is that I know so little about him, beyond his existence and the infinite patience and extent of his malignity. Examining what I do know, I write down:

> "He is a jailer.
> Allows me out on parole
> brings me back by telepathy
> is inside my mind
> breaks into my conversation with his own words
> speaking out of my mouth
> can overthrow me in a moment
> can be overthrown, if I have help
> writes with my hand, and censors what I write
> takes a dislike to my friends and sets me against them
> can take away pleasure
> is absent for long periods, shows up without notice
> employs disguise."

'If this is a game, it's past half-time and the beast winning. This isn't much help. Nor is the suggestion that he is:

> "A Mediaeval animal with a dog's face
> Notre Dame or Chartres is his proper place."

'I am afraid I know nothing about this beast at all: he is so amorphous and powerful that he could be a deity—only he is implacable; no use sacrificing to him, he takes what he wants.

> "Yes, I too have a particular monster
> a toad or a worm curled in the belly
> stirring, eating at times I cannot tell, he
> is the thing I can admit only once to
> anyone, never to those who have not their own,
> never to those who are happy."

'The quotations, of course, are from my own failures to write "Bête Noire".'

The present version of the poem is put together from four distinct fragments as indicated. An abandoned alternative to the opening of the third section reads:

> 'Yes, I too have a particular monster,
> a black lizard curled in my belly
> who stirs at times. I cannot tell.'

INDEX OF FIRST LINES